Better Homes and Gardens®

BEAUTIFUL KITCHENS™

WILEY

John Wiley & Sons, Inc.

Copyright © 2010 by Meredith Corporation, Des Moines, Iowa. All rights reserved

Published by John Wiley & Sons, Inc., Hoboken, New Jersey
Published simultaneously in Canada

For general information about our other products and services, please contact our Customer Care Department within the United States at (877) 762-2974, outside the United States at (317) 572-3993 or fax (317) 572-4002.

Wiley also publishes its books in a variety of electronic formats. Some content that appears in print may not be available in electronic books. For more information about Wiley products, visit our web site at www.wiley.com.

ISBN 978-0-470-50349-2

Printed in the United States of America

10 9 8 7 6 5 4 3 2 1

Note to the Readers:
Due to differing conditions, tools and the individual skills, John Wiley & Sons, Inc., assumes no responsibility for any damages, injuries suffered, or losses incurred as a result of following the information published in this book. Before beginning any project, review the instructions carefully, and if any doubts or questions remain, consult local experts or authorities. Because codes and regulations vary greatly, you always should check with authorities to ensure that your project complies with all applicable local codes and regulations. Always read and observe all of the safety precautions provided by manufacturers of any tools, equipment, or supplies, and follow all accepted safety procedures.

WELCOME

Some of life's most cherished moments happen in the kitchen. The small airings of bliss–rolling out cookie dough with a child, laughing with guests gathered around the island, or savoring a cup of tea in sunny solitude–are affirmations that the kitchen is the heart and soul of the home. It's no wonder, then, that we long for a kitchen that's wrapped in comfort and beauty yet still delivers the expected functionality. These kitchens, a compilation of some of the well-appointed rooms featured in *Beautiful Kitchens*™ magazine, offer inspiration that fulfills both goals. Utilitarian musts, such as ranges, sinks, and refrigerators, soar to dramatic new heights. Backsplashes sparkle with glass tile. Pendants–some sleek, others dripping with crystals–illuminate dining and work areas. Whatever your style, inspiration awaits within these pages. And when the simple pleasures that happen so naturally in a kitchen are given a beautiful backdrop, it's a recipe for success.

The Editors

Contents

6 Classic Elegance
8   Tradition with an Edge
14   Lighter, Brighter & Timeless
20   Regal Redux
26   Custom Blend
34   In Dark & Light

40 Relaxed Refinement
42   Cottage Sophisticate
50   Courting Character
56   A Soft Touch
62   Natural Embrace
70   Pastoral Suite

78 Sleek Sophistication
80   Modern Bliss
88   Pretty & Purposeful
96   Opposites Attract
102   A Place in the Sun

112 Global Influence
114   French Finesse
120   Culinary Haiku
128   Tuscan Tailored
134   With Spanish Eyes

142 Chef's Specials
144   Built on Experience
152   Heritage on Display
160   Metropolitan Medley
166   Function First
174   All Work & All Play
180   Double Feature

190   Resources

Classic

Elegance

Gracious styling and ornamentation bring an air of distinction into a kitchen. Flourishes, be they Gothic fretwork, gilt, or corbels, bespeak timelessness. Unexpected details are right at home too. Imagine a sleek chandelier bringing a modern edge to a traditional kitchen rich in mahogany. These rooms rise to the top in classic detailing that builds richness and depth.

Tradition with an Edge

This welcoming kitchen tailors the past in a crisp yet classic way.

Right: This kitchen puts a fresh spin on tradition by defining formal cabinetry with minimal detail: recessed and raised panels, ogee-edge brackets, and tapered and fluted columns. The contemporary chandelier glows with faux candlelight.

*J*ane Campbell and John McLeish built their Tudor-style home in the heart of Toronto. The architecture's blend of English and French influences suited their native city and the character of their established neighborhood. But that was no reason to copy the past in their kitchen.

The couple hired designer Brian Gluckstein, whose style, Jane says, "is classic enough to be comfortable, yet contemporary enough to be interesting." Gluckstein worked closely with their architect, Ray Murakami, during the initial planning stages to ensure that the kitchen design would complement the architecture's historical inspiration while suiting Jane and John's more contemporary needs and tastes.

Gothic arches in custom glass-front cabinets may mimic the detailing of antique furniture, but the kitchen's design is thoroughly modern. "We didn't want anything that appeared too new or too slick," Gluckstein says. "The overall look is crisp and clean, yet the wash on the cabinets is subtly off-white to add an appealing softness." Backsplashes are tiled in carrara marble; countertops are a smooth, gray, gently honed limestone reminiscent of traditional marble, with subtler veining for a more uniform surface. A chandelier also makes a playful nod to the past by casting a candle-light glow, although its look veers the furthest toward contemporary styles.

The focal point is a zinc range hood that bridges new and old. "The zinc relates especially well to the gleam of stainless-steel appliances and is quieter than traditional copper," Gluckstein says. Yet, like copper, the zinc hood should improve with age—acquiring the distinct character of its evolving patina.

This photo: Gothic-arch fretwork and ogee feet add furniture details to all-white cabinetry, creating the sense of a china hutch in proximity to the dining banquette.
Opposite: Inspired by library card catalogs, Jane Campbell uses these pullout drawers to corral recipes, matches, and small necessities.

Above left: The custom range hood combines a white-painted millwork frame, crisply edged ogee brackets, and built-in spice shelf that complement cabinetry with an acid-wash zinc cap. The zinc is fashioned into raised, spinelike joints to echo details on the home's Tudor exterior.
Above right: Unusually dense khaki-gray limestone countertops are finished with a 2-inch decorative ogee edge on the island. "With time, the limestone should acquire a wonderful patina like wood floors or vintage leather," designer Brian Gluckstein says.

Quartersawn oak floors with a natural-color stain also add warmth while unifying the kitchen with the house's other, more formal spaces. The floor plan, however, is geared to casual living. The 12×18-foot kitchen opens to the family room where a white coffered ceiling and built-in bookshelves blend seamlessly with views of kitchen cabinetry.

A hardworking island also unites the kitchen and family room. "Jane didn't want a lot of standing-around space in the kitchen," Gluckstein says. "Instead she wanted the island to be as large as possible and devoted to working." Clean, uncluttered countertops and a monochromatic palette keep the 5½×9-foot island from feeling too large in the space. The tapered and fluted square columns on the island's four corners minimize its bulk

while adding to the cohesive furniture look that makes a practical, and beautiful, connection between the kitchen and family room. "This way I can cook and compete with John's love for the Golf Channel," Jane says with a laugh.

Adding to the kitchen's comfort and versatility is a dining nook under a bay of windows, where a settee at the table creates the cozy effect of a banquette. "I'm adding a banquette to most of the kitchens I design these days," Gluckstein says, "They're much more comfortable than the traditional table-and-chair setup and are great for intimate meals when entertaining."

Gluckstein tailored the dining nook's window treatments to rhyme with the room's clean architecture: Side panels hanging in crisp columns, sheer Roman shades, and shutters for privacy frame the windows simply. The draperies and soft upholstery have the added benefit of absorbing sound amid the kitchen's many hard surfaces.

"We don't think we'll ever get tired of this kitchen," Jane says. "It's elegance with an edge." BK

dining

china

dw.

ref.

Opposite: A comfortable wingback settee creates the feel of a built-in banquette at the kitchen table. Window treatments in solid neutral colors are tailored in clean lines for a simplicity that does not detract from the beauty of the room's architecture, or views of English-style gardens.

This photo: White enamel paint brings crisp definition to the paneling of the range hood that was designed to complement the surrounding cabinetry.
Opposite: Celadon glazed backsplash tiles pop against the white porcelain apron-front sink and carrara marble countertops.

Lighter, Brighter & Timeless

Clean lines and bright white relax
a kitchen's heirloom character.

The possibilities were limitless. The designers of this recent project—a showhouse kitchen with no homeowners or budget to consider—had carte blanche to stock its generous space with an abundance of luxury materials, amenities, and furnishings. Instead, they deferred to a softer voice that cried out for reserve. The house itself dictated the design, says Kelly Welsh, a senior designer at Bellacasa Design Associates, the firm responsible for the kitchen design in this newly built home north of Houston.

The setting is a Normandy-style house hidden among native pines, where it appears to have stood for ages. Spacious yet comfortable in scale, the rooms are dressed with elegant reserve. "We approached the kitchen's interior in a similar fashion to the architecture to achieve a sense of timelessness and vintage appeal," says Kevin Spearman, designer and principal at the design firm.

"Simple, sophisticated, and nostalgic" was the mantra scribbled into the design team's notebook as they toured the home during construction. They imagined the room in a vintage East Coast vernacular, Welsh says; in particular, they wished to emulate the stately simplicity of early-20th-century homes that line the coast from Rhode Island to the Hamptons.

Above left: Chicken-wire-front bookcases flank the paneled refrigerator for a furniture look.
This photo: Hand-glazed celadon wall tiles extend their subtle sheen from countertop height to the 12-foot-high ceiling, drawing eyes to the soaring proportions of the cabinetry and the central arched window.

Left: The built-in china cabinet in the dining room takes its style cues from the cabinetry of the adjacent butler's pantry and kitchen. Right: Planned as a corridor between the kitchen and dining room, the butler's pantry allows access to fulfill entertaining needs. An arch midway divides the cleanup and beverage-station areas with stately character.

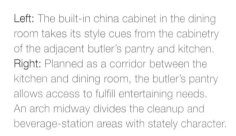

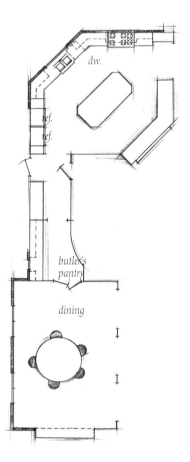

The sheen of white enamel paint and white carrara marble countertops was key to the team's goal of a light and airy classic look. Both reflect streaming morning sunlight from a large, gracefully arched above-sink window, which is the room's focal point and inspiration. Glass-front cabinets also amplify light and, combined with open vertical plate storage, bring vintage aesthetics into play. The heirloom look continues in the dining room, which is accessed from the kitchen through the corridor-style butler's pantry.

The decision to not place a sink in the center island keeps kitchen prep off display and ensures the room always looks neat, Welsh says. Countertops are reserved for food preparation, she explains, so the island can serve as a focal point and additional serving space. Its dark-stained base—customized to resemble furniture—appears weightier, anchoring the cooler colors of the room.

"Because of its shape and size, the kitchen lends itself to extra hands," says Welsh, who imagined the space accommodating everything from friends preparing casual meals together to catered events. That vision helped shape the room's flow in terms of both layout and mood. From the kitchen to the pantry to the dining room and beyond, teak floors and crisp white millwork present an understated elegance. "We envisioned clean lines and a sense of lightness," Spearman says. "There was no place here for heavy, contrived formality."

This photo: Hand-finished cabinets with gold-leaf trim mimic the look of fine Continental antiques. The mahogany island echoes the dark wood of an upper-level wine vault visible from the kitchen.
Opposite: Inset tile backsplashes with a herringbone pattern make a natty contrast to the marble counters and trim.

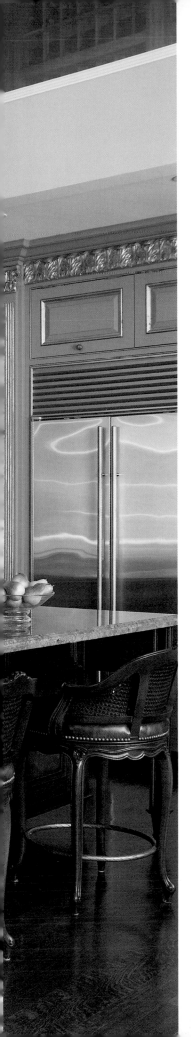

Regal Redux

A touch of gold dresses
cabinetry in the kitchen
of a historic home.

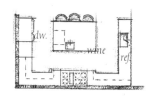

Left: An elegant new bridge faucet suits the home's age and serves a stainless-steel sink set under the creamy marble counter.
Below: The island's red marble countertop departs from the lighter marble of perimeter counters to bring out the rich hues of the mahogany base.

*U*pdating a nearly century-old kitchen poses a serious question: whether to convey some sense of the age and original architecture or to begin literally anew with modern style and convenience. The most satisfying solution typically lies between, as it did in this circa-1910 home in Toronto's Forest Hill neighborhood. Architect/designer Dee Dee Hannah devised the space for a serious cook, convivial entertainer, and mother of three—who insisted on a formal kitchen as beautiful as her historic home and its fine period furniture, but with up-to-the-minute function.

"That's what's so fun about today's kitchens," Hannah says. "They can convey a lovely aesthetic feel and be high-performing." In this case, a large part of that expert function lies in expanded space. The new kitchen is part of an addition that replaced the original 12×15-foot space with a 16×20-foot working kitchen open to an elegant breakfast area and hearthside family room.

The style of the kitchen echoes the Georgian style of the home. It's also largely inspired by a particular shade of green, which the homeowner admired on the pages of a magazine several years earlier. Hannah introduced a sea of hand-finished green cabinets accented in lustrous gold leaf. "The new kitchen, breakfast area, and family room really have a French feel in their detailing," she explains.

The cabinet finish involved a four-step process of painting and antiquing the doors, then adding gold leaf and toning it down. Gilt ovals appear on cabinet doors, and appliquéd gilt carving replicates the ornate band that wraps the upper kitchen cabinets. A trio of antique chandeliers with dangling crystal fruit continues the elegance, illuminating the island as well as the breakfast area.

All these cook-friendly features cloaked in sumptuous classicism prove that the answer to the question—whether to look back or look forward—can be simple: both. ⊕

The visual weight of the stately dark mahogany island, dark barstools, and wide-plank oak flooring keeps the painted and gilt-touched kitchen from appearing too fragile for its function.

In Detail

Achieving a rich look on the cabinetry was as involved as finishing a fine piece of furniture. Here's the strategy behind the spectacular results.

Opposite: A mahogany base anchors the island against fields of green. Its reddish brown stain blends with rosy marble countertops and grows darker in the recesses of moldings to suggest age.

Clockwise from top left: The cupboards began as a dark pistachio, which was antiqued on-site with a brush coat of a gray-tone French green. The resulting shade is richer and deeper, helping to ease the shine of gilt on oval medallions and bands of acanthus leaf trim. • The gold leaf was selectively applied to enhance the relief of carvings, then toned down to mimic the lesser shine of an antique. • A thin band of antiqued gilt molding matches ornate, furniture-style hardware on the narrow drawers that provide handy pantry space inside columns flanking the mantel hood.

Style cues ranging from turn-of-the-century artisan to Hollywood chic beautifully mix in this kitchen.

Custom Blend

Gathering is key to this kitchen. A dining table anchors the lively concoction of styles and materials, extending from pro-style stainless-steel appliances to a dignified marble and granite floor and paint-glazed country cabinetry.

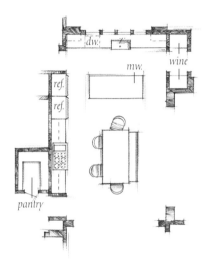

Right: Decorative brackets support upper cabinets to frame the cooking niche.
Opposite: The pro-style, stainless-steel range, with its own backsplash, and a corrugated steel vent hood in the shape of a storefront awning add industrial counterpoint to walls and counters clad in slabs of marble.

Moving breezily from coast to coast and decade to decade, this kitchen's style is impossible to pigeonhole. "We aimed for a look of Hamptons Arts and Crafts blended with Hollywood diner," homeowner Brian Thompson says. Traditional green-glazed woodwork and furnishings play against a checkerboard floor and an awning-style range hood fashioned in corrugated stainless steel.

"The fun lies in juxtaposing styles and materials," says Brian, a builder by occupation. "The 'If one thing is pewter, then everything is pewter' idea is not for us." Instead he and his wife, Katherine, let Brian's penchant for play guide their kitchen's distinctive design.

His talent for mixing, and improvising, shows in the standout checkerboard floor. The white squares are carrara marble, the contrasting squares black granite. "Black marble wasn't available, but I found the granite has the same look," he says. Brian had doubts about a highly graphic floor pattern at first but now loves its "old Hollywood feel"—a touch of drama in a mostly subdued kitchen.

The couple's lighthearted approach to their kitchen extended to their home's exterior. They installed runs of windows, French doors, and transoms at every opportunity to balance the heavy English-style stone facade. In brilliantly sunny Houston, northern exposure seemed just right for a window expanse over the kitchen sink. This put the light-filled work area at the cooler end of the space and a sunroom-cum-family room at the warm, south-facing end.

"The kitchen is close to 50 feet by 20 feet," Brian says. "We can get a lot of activity into that space with three children and Bear, our teacup poodle. Nearly 80 percent of our time is spent here."

The Thompsons' first thought was to have two islands

Nooks above the refrigerators house a collection of white ceramics. The decorative effect helps balance the room's mix of work and cozy dining zones.

and to place a dining area where the sunroom is now. "Then we put our dining table in the middle of the room," Brian says. Siting the table in place of a second island turned a potentially cavernous space into a warm, inviting room.

A maple top helps the island blend with the dining table, while lighting distinguishes each surface. An industrial-style metal pendant offers downlight over the island, while a crystal chandelier hangs over the table. Other surprising pairings include the vintage Franklin range and the microwave drawer in the island. "It's cool," Brian says of the high-tech drawer. "Just push a button and 'shzzzzz'—out it glides."

Twin dishwashers on either side of the sink help with housekeeping. "And a nook off the kitchen has a wine cooler so we don't need to wander far for entertaining," Brian says.

"The room has great flow," he adds. In addition to ample work areas, "There's plenty of what I call standing-around areas. Even with a full house, we're never crowded." 🅱🅺

Above: The sink is set off by a wide bank of windows above and china cabinets on either side. Glass on two sides allows views into the cabinets from the sink or from across the room.
Left: A microwave drawer tucks conveniently into the island.
Opposite: Carrara marble dresses countertops around the stainless-steel double sink with its industrial sprayer/faucet combo.

In Dark & Light

Two zones
with distinct
palettes define
this cozy kitchen.
One celebrates
the room's
traditional roots;
the other, its
contemporary
convenience.

Designer Brian Gluckstein styled his kitchen with inspiration from vintage libraries. "I wanted it to feel as if I put a kitchen in the library," he says.

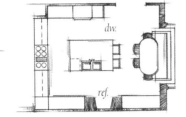

Opposite: Brian designed the custom range hood with a lip for cookbooks and a blackboard finish that accommodates household notes or favorite recipes.
Right: White carrara marble countertops, matching mosaic marble-clad walls, and open shelves made of marble slabs add a luxe touch, while cubbies inspired by card catalogs bring casual appeal.

Mahogany speaks a classical language, says designer Brian Gluckstein, who chose richly stained expanses of the wood to convey a sense of tradition in the redesign of his Toronto kitchen. His plan took inspiration from vintage libraries, which he emulated in the handsome styling of the Gothic fretwork of glass-front cabinets and in detailed moldings.

But dark mahogany was hardly suited to the windowless walls allocated for the range and other appliances. Neither was the wood's traditional aesthetic an ideal choice to project the cooking area's contemporary efficiency. "Vintage libraries look as good today as the day they were built, but if I did the entire room in mahogany it would be too dark," he says.

Instead, Brian transitioned his kitchen from dark to light, using a crisp white palette for cabinets, countertops, and open shelving on opposite walls. Juxtaposing white paint with dark stain on cabinets added a relaxed, more informal component, as well as a clear division between cooking and entertaining zones.

The floor plan achieves two goals: It makes a focal point of the mahogany built-ins that are open to the home's main hall and family room, while hiding the utilitarian part of the kitchen from around-the-clock views. "I didn't want guests to sit in the family room and have to look at the kitchen sink," Brian says. "It was important that the long wall have beautiful mahogany cabinetry with the elegance of a breakfront or fine furniture."

This distinction of placement—and atmosphere—carries through to the kitchen's finer details. The mahogany wall celebrates tradition with a prominent hearth and antique brass-finish cabinet hardware, while the work zone's fresh white paint, smooth nickel cabinet pulls, and floating marble shelves create a more contemporary silhouette.

Compatible materials, surfaces, and finishes balance the different looks of dual zones. For example, two varieties of honed marble—rich brown-black on the central island and a white-veined version on the oven wall countertops

and backsplash—share a rich patina and a classical countenance. "The deep brown marble on the island harmonizes well with the mahogany wall, while the white in the work zone adds a softness that relates well to the creamy white-painted cabinets," Brian says.

An oversize island with a rich mahogany base that matches the cabinets visually anchors the two zones. Designed as the kitchen's focal point and main prep area, the island also allowed Brian to avoid perimeter counters and cabinets on two walls that could have boxed in the space. Because Brian and his partner entertain frequently—dinner parties often include impromptu cooking classes by local chefs—the island also accommodates a number of cooks.

"Multiple cooks can work on both sides or even side by side," Brian says. "It allows us to really interact with our guests while preparing and cooking a meal."

Near the island is an elegant dining nook with the kitchen's single window—a bay that bathes the space in natural light. The nook, which overlooks a lush, English-style garden, is a favored place for evening dinners and lazy Sunday brunches. Though the kitchen can easily handle a crowd, it is also perfect for more intimate entertaining. "We love relaxing with the newspaper and coffee in the morning or having a few friends over for a meal by the fire," Brian says.

Many of those friends remark on the kitchen when they visit for the first time.

"People walk down the hall and see the fireplace wall first and say, 'Oh, how beautiful,'" Brian says. "It's only after they walk into the room that they realize it's a kitchen." 🅱🅚

Relaxed

Refinement

*E*stablish an easygoing manner with a kitchen that's short on pomp and long on comfort. Think cottage charm or country rusticity, fixtures that wear an aged patina, and rough-hewn surfaces. Or temper the formality of classic design with slipcovered chairs or weathered beams on ceilings. In these kitchens, relaxed touches contribute a special stay-awhile allure.

This photo: A classic red-and-white color scheme climaxes in a jazzy checkerboard-pattern tile backsplash above the range. **Opposite:** Homeowner Carlene Condon wanted ample views of her gardens incorporated into the new kitchen's architectural plan.

Cottage Sophisticate

A seaside kitchen is stylish,
smooth-functioning, and simply
smashing in red.

This photo: Cabinets feature doors of varying panel styles for a gathered look. Wood knobs, countertops, and floors add a sense of warmth and age to support the kitchen's vintage cottage inspiration.
Opposite: A picnic-check cushion and mismatched pillows on the window seat echo the color scheme with carefree charm.

*F*red and Carlene Condon had a new life in mind when they moved with their twin daughters from the stresses of suburbia to the dream home they built on a plot of island real estate. Time for family, cooking, and gardening was the focus of their move—as well as the inspiration for the comforts attained in their new kitchen's design.

But while the couple wanted a kitchen suited to their new low-key lifestyle, they hoped for a look more elegant than what is often found in cottage-style design. Architect Patrick Ahearn and kitchen designer Beverly Ellsley honored their request with a room that's far from staid thanks to charming furniture details and a cheerful smattering of red.

Varying shades of red show up on the base of a central island and its stools, in the color of the French range, and in a bold checkerboard-pattern tile backsplash above the range. Cherrywood is added selectively—on the island countertop, on the break-front bookcases that flank a window seat, and on a bank of perimeter cabinets—in order to blend with the vibrant hue while adding an all-season sense of warmth to the scheme of contrasting brights.

Six coats of oil-base urethane sealer lend the cherrywood countertops a high-polish look while protecting from moisture and stains. "I'm fond of wood countertops," Ellsley says. "I've had them in my own home for 30 years. They're lovely and durable." Occasional burns or scratches in the wood are simply sanded out, she says.

Sunny yellow beaded-board walls balance the red-painted surfaces and cherrywood accents. All hues are set against the backbone of the room's cottage-style design—a surround of white-painted cabinets with oversize round wood knobs. "Playing with scale is one way to create a cottage look for cabinetry," Ellsley says. "Larger stiles and rails on doors work to create a more informal look."

Ellsley also added eclectic touches to enhance the personality of her cottage design. She planned cabinets with a mix of rectangular, square, and oblong recessed panels as well as occasional plain fronts and glass inserts. Brackets, scrolled feet, and a pair of bifold doors pierced in a trellis pattern add layers of elegant tradition to the more carefree juxtaposition of door fronts.

Above left: A farmhouse sink in the cleanup zone is flanked by marble countertops and soaked in light from a wide arch-top window.
Left: The red island and yellow beaded-board walls contrast in hue while sharing a degree of warmth. Both stand out against a perimeter of white-painted cabinets.
Opposite: Cabinets mimic freestanding furniture with elegant bracket feet, glass-pane doors, and rich cherry countertops.

Windows, thoughtfully sited by Ahearn, further enhance the room's charm. They interrupt walls of storage with elegantly framed views of the ocean, Carlene's gardens, and the children's outdoor play areas.

Generous exterior views cater to the kitchen zones in most frequent use. The island faces a bank of windows fit with a cozy window seat, for example, while a windowed alcove with seaside views functions as the main cleanup area. The room's only small, round window is more about style than vistas, however: adds panache to a bank of glass-front cabinets that store special-occasion tableware.

A pair of hand-painted doors is the final touch in this kitchen where nothing is uniform, nothing is dull, and all appears to have been collected over time. 🄱🄺

WHERE'S THE EXTRA OVEN?

"In the cupboard," says designer Beverly Ellsley, who hid the kitchen's second-string appliances for these reasons:
FREQUENCY OF USE: It's not every day that the family uses a second oven or the microwave. So why design all in plain view?
NOSTALGIC CHARM: Cottage style harks back to simpler times when one oven was enough—a value better displayed by the classic look of the European range than a sleek, stainless-steel oven or microwave.

This photo: Antique doors hand-painted with florals create an elegant passage from the kitchen to the family's primary dining space.
Opposite top: Careful planning provided views into the fireside dining space for cooks working at the island or the range.
Opposite bottom: An arched bookshelf holding Carlene's cookbook collection is built into one side of the refrigerator cabinet.

Clapboard walls and a muted, Colonial-inspired palette of white and gray add timeless character to this modern cottage kitchen.

Courting Character

Cottage dressings harmonize with streamlined simplicity in a new kitchen filled with vintage inspiration.

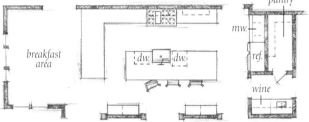

pantry

mw.

breakfast area

dw. dw.

ref.

wine

Homeowners Gary and Amy Dresser dreamed of a kitchen that was easy on the eyes—and on the cook. Their elegant Atlanta manor house, completed in the summer of 2006, includes this 340-square-foot kitchen. "We both like to cook and both wanted a refined, timeless look," Gary says. What that entailed, however, meant something different to this husband and wife.

Gary defined his style as clean-lined, orderly, and elegant, while Amy wished for more of an English cottage feel. With the help of a local architect, the couple found their ideal in an uncluttered design that mixes in classic cottage elements. The result is great flexibility. Here, along with their two children, the couple enjoy whipping up a light snack or entertaining a formal party of 12 in the same space.

Much relies on a clever footprint and savvy storage. "We wanted this to be an open kitchen that invites people in to interact with the hostess without getting into her work space," architect David Fowler says. He created a galley layout that places the range, sink, and refrigerator just steps from each

other. "We were a little concerned that there wouldn't be enough space to freely move about, but it turned out to be a very efficient layout—a work center for the cook and a very large area for entertaining," Fowler says.

The homeowners commissioned a local crafter to build the cabinets, complete with soft-close hinges. For cottage-inspired charm, all millwork was coated in gray lacquer, including bracket shelves for open storage, which Fowler recommended in lieu of upper cabinets to help visually expand the room.

This meant that base cabinets had to be especially efficient. Fowler planned for deep drawers to hold cookware, glassware, and kitchen utensils. He even took a thorough inventory of the family's various small appliances, wine glasses, and tools to ensure everything would have a place.

Next to the stainless-steel refrigerator, a bank of cabinets accommodates a microwave surrounded by small drawers filled with tea, spices, and linens. A walk-in pantry behind the refrigerator wall provides ample storage for food and

This photo: Dishwashers flank the deep farmhouse sink on the island, creating an efficient zone for cleanup.
Opposite left: Cottage-style touches include stacked bracket shelves painted to contrast with white clapboard walls.
Opposite right: Open shelves for cookbooks minimize the heft of the island.

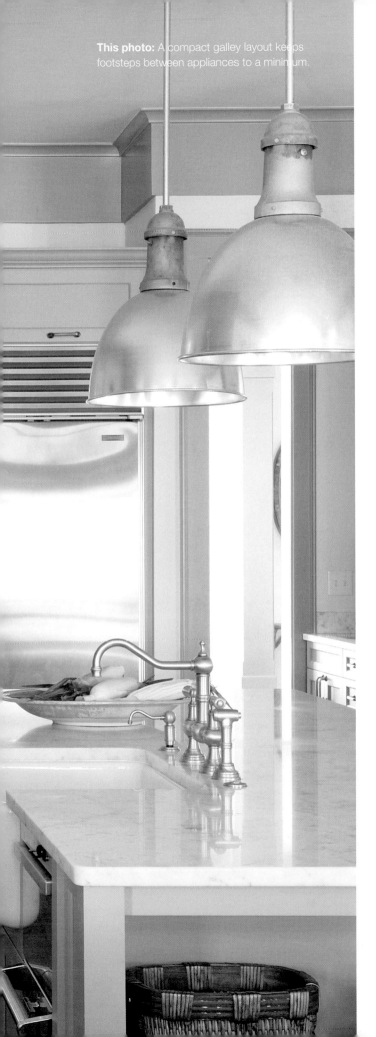

This photo: A compact galley layout keeps footsteps between appliances to a minimum.

WHAT GOES WHERE

Cabinets around the microwave are custom-sized to store items handy to this appliance and the adjacent refrigerator. "It's our snack station," homeowner Gary Dresser says. "We can make lunch for the kids there and pack it to go."

Three small drawers stacked in a column hold items that tend to get lost in larger drawers: tea bags, straws, and markers to label lunch bags.

A wide drawer is sized to hold plastic wrap and baggies used in the microwave or in lunch packs.

Two shallow drawers below the ledge serve as catchalls. "One is the junk drawer," Gary says. "Everyone needs one." The other stores disposable plastic flatware and napkins.

Lower cabinets store lunch boxes, beverage carriers, and plastic storage bowls used for leftovers in the fridge or snacks on the go.

larger serving pieces. "We ended up with so much room, some of our cabinets are still empty," Gary says.

Work space is also plentiful for the family of hobby cooks. The ample peninsula proves a great place for chopping or baking, while the island houses sink tasks. Honed Italian marble countertops unite the zones.

Although the kitchen opens to the foyer and the living space, the Dressers wanted enough wall space to display artwork. Simple 1×10-inch shiplap siding, painted white, becomes a neutral backdrop for art with historical character.

Sunshine pours into the kitchen most mornings as the kids enjoy a quick breakfast at the island. The family takes evening meals at the country French table, but even then it's a casual affair. "When all the neighbor kids are over, we'll order a pizza and there's plenty of room for everyone to sit and socialize," Gary says. "We love it."

A Soft Touch

Pretty pastel hues and winsome carvings relax a hardworking yet elegant kitchen.

This photo: Kitchen cabinets and trim are designed to blend into a wainscoting surround. The transom-topped doorway, leading to one of two pantries that flank the commercial-grade refrigerator, also extends the millwork's crisp style.

Opposite: A bowl fashioned from rough-hewn stone plays against the sleek elegance of a white lava-stone countertop and crystal pulls on the island.

A kitchen's demand for hard surfaces—cabinets, countertops, and washable floors—seldom translates to a soft, cozy space for living. But Andrea and John Moran, the owners behind this vintage-inspired kitchen remodel, were insistent on taking a light approach. The couple had brightened the dark mahogany paneling of their stately 1906 red brick home in St. Louis's prestigious Central West End neighborhood with a quick coat of crisp white paint, but faced much more than cosmetic changes to transform their kitchen from its lackluster past. Enter architect Stanley McKay, who helped give the room its fresh start.

Despite the home's overall elegance, decades of remodels had obliterated the kitchen's period character—that is, if it ever had any to save. Kitchens in homes of this period often were no more than bare-bones, utilitarian spaces for servants, McKay says. This time around, the challenge was twofold: to remake the room as a living and entertaining space equipped for an active, modern family and to impart the same level of understated elegance befitting the rest of the home's interior.

After gutting the kitchen, McKay began by wrapping walls in white-painted, deeply paneled wainscoting similar to woodwork found in other rooms. "It adds substantial texture," he says. The same wainscoting was fashioned into a pair of tall pantry cabinets that flank the commercial-grade range and its stainless-steel countertops. "We wanted to bring storage into the kitchen in a way that was

Above: A gracefully arched faucet pairs with spray handles and a drinking-water tap—all in vintage style with a gleaming nickel finish.
Opposite: Three dishwashers are built into one side of the island. The design leaves three sides open to island dining thanks to its extended white lava-stone countertop and elegantly carved column legs.

appropriate for the character of the space," McKay says. "Wall-mounted cabinets, we thought, would scream re-model and would look out of place. These units imply the kitchen has been there forever."

Aesthetics and comfort remained a focus equal to the kitchen's high-function requirements. While storage, cooking, and prep have their own dedicated zones, McKay was careful to allocate a full third of the original space, as well as a new window-lined alcove, for seating. "We wanted the kitchen to be a bright, light hangout space for our family and friends," Andrea says.

The kitchen island extends on three sides to make room for casual counter seating, while pretty slipcovers on dining chairs allow for a more stylish gathering. Pillows and cushions on the carved settee also take advantage of easy-care slipcovers for a softer, more casual look than permanent upholstery. "Slipcovers just look homey to me," Andrea says. "They're like comfortable clothes for furniture."

Although the grand style of the home dictated some formalities, nothing overshadowed the family's desire for a friendly, comfortable space. Crystal pulls and elegant column legs on the island and a glass chandelier over the kitchen table set a refined tone that is tempered in proximity to the everyday utility of stainless steel. And though marble was clearly an option for its milky-white color and sheen, McKay opted to top the island with white enamel glazed lava stone. Absent of veining, its surface appears bright and clean and is easy for the active family to maintain.

Another inventive surface was used for the backsplash above the dual-oven range. The brick-size tiles are Vitrolite, a kind of glass sometimes found on storefronts from the 1930s, McKay says. "It's another material intended to make the kitchen feel different, less predictable than, say, ceramic subway tiles." Andrea also enjoys its unique practicality. "There isn't a single surface that I can't clean with Windex and paper towels," she says.

Flooring is the kitchen's finishing touch. Marble square tiles set in a border pattern add another layer of style and character. Honed stone conveys a sense of age, while the pattern's diagonal direction manipulates perspective to build an impression of spaciousness. The modern needs and traditional appeal of this kitchen come together with a welcome new style that maintains its respect for the past. ●

Natural Embrace

This cottage kitchen in a converted
boat shed evokes the materials and
colors of its seaside locale.

This photo: Crustaceans inhabit a stunning range backsplash that combines gray-green Arts and Crafts tile with copper insets.
Opposite: The green marble countertops feature a subtly undulating surface with an organic feel that complements the evolving patina on a copper farmhouse sink.

Sitting in the architectural shell that would become a kitchen in a home on Nantucket Island, designer Jean Courtney was bathed in shadow even in front of windows. Beyond, however, lay a wind-ruffled wetland and a pond that mirrored the open sky. "I wanted to bring that feeling inside and create a kitchen that would feel warm and sunny, but still fresh, like a summer breeze," Courtney says. "The room faces northwest, so there's no light until 2 p.m. I knew I had to add light however I could."

Her solution was to drench the room in color. Instead of using a white-and-blue palette—"which almost everyone does here," she says—Courtney chose cabinetry with a custard-yellow finish to radiate warmth. She picked yellow for the walls and ceiling, too, adding a rich brown glaze for old-world flavor. For cool contrast, the kitchen island wears a sgraffito (or scratched) teal finish that subtly recalls the sea. "The design is all about the environment," Courtney says.

Originally a barn and boat shed, the house was recently transformed into a cedar-shingle cottage by architect Lyman Perry. "They used to repair boats where the kitchen is now," Courtney says. The new home combines a relaxed rusticity with traditional style. Old pine planks lie underfoot, weathered beams (many of them decorative) stretch overhead, and a massive stone fireplace presents its back to the kitchen. Courtney's colorful plan for the kitchen had to rhyme with this natural scheme.

Right: An homage to sun and sea, this kitchen features a palette of yellow, teal, and sea-moss green with copper accents. Rope-turned pilasters on cabinets add elegance to the casual Nantucket theme.

She chose hand-painted alder cabinets featuring such furniture details as rope-style pilasters and beaded face frames. The French cast-iron range is a lucky find virtually identical in color to the cabinets.

Perimeter countertops are green marble with a honed, undulating surface. "They're not perfectly smooth," Courtney says. "They're a little wavy, but you can put anything on them—your cup or wineglass isn't going to fall over. It's a very beautiful, very natural surface, and it emulates the sea." The countertops' simple, squared-off pencil edge lets the stone be the focus.

The island's multilayer finish has a hint of verdigris, so Courtney knew copper would be a perfect accent—one she lavishly applied throughout the room. "The copper adds light and texture," she says. The 3×6-foot island features a copper

This photo: Light reflections single out the hammered copper sink from the smooth, copper-topped island. **Opposite top:** One cabinet holds two slender refrigerators set side-by-side. **Opposite bottom:** A microwave oven tucks neatly under the counter beside wine cubbies that capitalize on slender storage space.

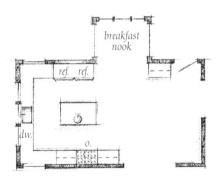

countertop, as well as a hammered copper sink. The large apron-front sink in the cleanup zone is copper, too, as are the faucets. Finally, copper insets embellish a tile mural above the range.

Some might fear the upkeep of copper—especially on a countertop—but that's not a problem, Courtney says. "There are so many cleaning products available today that copper is fine for everyday use," she says. Now three years old, the island top has the lovely patina of a well-worn penny. Copper is not a good cutting surface, however, so Courtney parked a rolling butcher-block cart at one end of the island and stocked the cabinets with plenty of cutting boards.

A broad bank of windows, a large range hood, and built-ins for the two refrigerators left few opportunities for wall cabinets. Even so, the 15×18-foot room is packed with easy-access storage. Deep drawers at one end of the island

hold everyday plates, just a quick turn from the dishwasher. Close by—opposite the refrigerators and microwave—more island cabinets stow cups and everyday glassware. "It's arranged so you can get something to drink, or heat something up in the microwave, without interfering with the cooking area," Courtney says. "This kitchen easily accommodates two cooks."

The room takes full advantage of its island setting, even when fog shrouds the coastline. "Inside this kitchen, I feel alive and happy," Courtney says. "It's really refreshing." 🅱🅺

Opposite: The breakfast nook, sited in a bay between the refrigerators and a beverage center, features a table and chairs that match the teal finish on the island and window trim.
Above left: Part coffee station, part wine bar, a built-in sideboard by the breakfast nook includes an undercounter wine chiller.
Above right: Glass fronts on island drawers reveal seashells for decoration along with glimpses of dry goods and linens.

This photo: Cabinets use at least five species of wood and four kinds of stone. Surfaces vary for reasons of beauty and function, ranging from a hardworking granite-top island to its elegant counterpart, a second island finished in olive green with gold leaf trim.
Opposite: The kitchen's prep and cleanup sinks feel cohesive with identical faucets and parallel placement.

Pastoral Suite

A few rustic touches bring a comfortable country quality to a sophisticated kitchen.

This photo: The cleanup area is elegant and efficient with a marble apron sink, flanking glass-front upper cabinets for tableware display, as well as an icemaker, undercounter refrigerator, and dishwasher in cabinets below.
Right: An ebonized walnut beverage center hides countertop appliances behind a mirrored-panel backsplash.

Offering equal parts finery and farmhouse comfort, Debbie and Fred Schwartz's 150-year-old estate is a distinctive mix of sophistication and easy living. The lush property hosts horses, gardens, and rolling forest, as well as a glimpse of the Wisconsin state capitol building located just minutes away in downtown Madison. Call it high-country style or kicked-back urbanism, the Schwartzes' lifestyle continues to rest on a strong connection to the land and its traditions—neither of which was served by the sleek white-on-white kitchen that a 1980s remodel had buried deep within the house.

The Schwartzes wanted a new kitchen to connect to the outdoors and to reflect their taste for European-style refinements. Initially, the couple and their designer, Chicago-based Mick De Giulio, considered tearing down a family room addition on the back of the home and building a new kitchen in its place. In the end, however, they converted the existing addition into a gracious suite that combines kitchen functions with a well-furnished gathering space.

During the renovation, windows were enlarged and repositioned to better frame views. An elegantly scaled bump-out

Black and white marble tile runs the length of the kitchen/family room conversion, connecting the suite's various zones with a swath of brasserie style.

for casual dining extends views of the property's old-growth oaks and maples. "I wanted to know I'd always feel tuned in to the outside in this room," Debbie says.

But openness can have its challenges. De Giulio had a beamed ceiling lowered over work areas to tame the potentially cavernous space. The vaulted ceiling resumes at the far end of the suite, where plush seating surrounds a fireplace and overmantel, flat-panel television. There the ceiling boards are painted a light-reflecting white between richly stained beams to balance the Schwartzes' new aerie with its patina of history. "The kitchen couldn't feel tacked on," De Giulio says. "We had to find a way to preserve the intimate and charming architecture of the old farmhouse."

Assigning kitchen functions to a double-galley layout with designated zones suits the extra-long dimensions of the converted space. Two islands—a larger island topped with granite and a smaller island painted olive green, trimmed in gold leaf, and topped with brown fossil stone—are centered to facilitate traffic to and from the dining and gathering spaces beyond. A beverage center, complete with chilled wine storage and dish cleanup zone, are sited out of the way to ensure the kitchen can graciously host larger gatherings.

WHY MIX MATERIALS?

It's key to a well-furnished look and distinct work zones, says designer Mick De Giulio.

WOODS: *Establish a tonal range* The most comfortable living spaces appear collected over time, and kitchens are no exception. Using a range of wood finishes gives built-ins the look of gathered furniture.

STONES: *Add midtone hues* Countertops and backsplashes offer occasion to enrich the tonal range of cabinets. Try surfaces that are close in color, but that add rich texture.

HIGHS AND LOWS: *Finish with contrast* Juxtaposing bright and dark colors, as these homeowners did on their checkered floor, creates high drama.

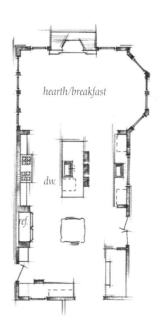

Within the kitchen galley, De Giulio designed a series of furniturelike cabinet units, mixing exquisite finishes and a surprising number of materials (see "Why Mix Materials?", page 75). "Each area, each piece, is its own element rather than the expected continuum where everything matches," De Giulio says. The refrigerator is wrapped in mesquite with routed door panels and an arched top to resemble a Georgian armoire, for example, while the black-glazed beverage center with leaded-glass doors and a white marble countertop takes its style cues from British manor homes.

Complementary hues bring consistency to the room's range of materials. Woods are combined for both beauty (cherry in the central island; butternut on selected drawers and doors) and function (a teak chopping area; glazed walnut cabinets near sinks). A similarly inspiring range of stone includes scoon, a refined French limestone, around the range and a classic grid of black and white marble floor tile for contrast—both "perfectly suited to the couple's continental-meets-country aesthetic," De Giulio says. ◼

hearth/breakfast

dw.

ref.

Opposite: A vaulted ceiling opens up the far end of the kitchen suite, which includes upholstered chairs for fireside reading, conversation, and watching television.
This photo: A small bump-out is fitted with banquette seating and a custom-designed table that comfortably seats up to six for breakfast, snacks, or casual meals.

Sleek Sop

sophistication

Smooth surfaces, clean lines, fluid curves. These are hallmarks of kitchens that embrace simplicity in design and architecture. Stripped of ornamentation, every element–the arch of a faucet or the gleam of stainless steel–becomes sculptural. For understated beauty and uncluttered efficiency, take a cue from these streamlined spaces.

Modern Bliss

Sleek silhouettes create a
contemplative space inspired
by beautiful views.

This sophisticated, modern kitchen still
feels cozy thanks to a combination of clean
lines and warm, neutral colors.

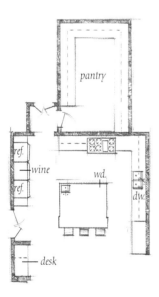

Broad vistas of the colorful Marin Hills led Shawn and Matt Gillam to design their new home with its environs in mind—even in a kitchen with no windows of its own. Pale oak cabinets with a horizontal grain stop short of the ceiling, creating serene, contemporary lines that reflect the natural beauty of the land with minimal visual distraction.

"We love to cook and entertain," Shawn says, "so we wanted to keep the kitchen simple and open. It had to be calming and sophisticated, yet it also had to be a place where even our kids could feel comfortable." Opting to finish their kitchen themselves, the Gillams conjured the same Zen-like air here as in the rest of the home, which project designer Michael Palza fashioned as a seamless expanse of living space enveloped by the landscape.

"I basically gave Shawn a blank canvas," Palza says of the two-walled kitchen that opens to living areas where dramatic views are the focus. "The key was positioning the kitchen so its views are outward rather than inward." The Gillams placed the island where a cook can take in expansive views from adjoining rooms. And on the windowless walls they employed a variety of natural materials, including oak

Opposite: Three appliances—a refrigerator, wine cooler, and freezer—are integrated into cabinets. Each appliance's drawers are paneled, while their stainless-steel doors are exposed.
This photo: Sheets of stainless steel create a sleek, easy-clean backsplash behind the range, a 48-inch model chosen for its simple lines and convenient double oven.

Right: The stainless-steel backsplash rises higher behind the range, where it's most needed, and drops significantly around perimeter cabinets.

Opposite: Frosted-glass cabinet doors seem to float over the sink counter, adding an ethereal note to ample storage.

Below: An undermount sink eases the smooth transition between wood, metal, and stone.

cabinets and lava rock countertops, to buttress the organic feel and soften the largely minimalist style.

"I love the look of modern, but I also have two children," Shawn says. "I was originally thinking of concrete work surfaces and lots of stainless steel, but then I had my first baby and thought, *Wow, that's really impractical.*" With a robust balance of clean lines and warm textures, Shawn maintains the crispness she desired while still building a friendly and inviting atmosphere.

Her secret? Clever contrasts. Against a backdrop of pecan-color walls and ceilings, she and Matt chose ebony-stained floors. To rival the richness of their gray-tone Italian basalt counters, they selected pale oak cabinetry cut on a horizontal grain. They also balanced heavy with light, tempering the island's heft with wispy steel barstools of Shawn's design.

This clean, elegant aesthetic is nearly impossible without one secret weapon: a pantry. The Gillams' walk-in is the true workhorse of their kitchen, keeping dry goods and other essentials out of sight but still easily accessible. "I don't think you can have a sleek, modern kitchen, especially one with so few walls, and not have a pantry," Shawn says. "It really

BACKSPLASHES
don't have to extend from counters to cabinets. This light valance tops the backsplash for modern flair, while discreetly concealing electrical outlets.

allowed us to focus on form in the public part of the room, and keep clutter very much under control."

Shawn insisted on having no visible outlets along her kitchen backsplash. Instead, she designed an ingenious stainless-steel valance that conceals several plug-ins and sheds a band of light. The valance serves as a visual place marker, tying the stove area to the rest of the work surface and echoing the horizontal lines of the cabinetry.

"I'm against stuff, or at least seeing it laid out all the time," Shawn says. "So for this kitchen, I wanted to get the basics in place—everything we needed to cook a good meal or entertain friends—and then let the architecture do its work.

"I wouldn't call it jet-setting or ultrasophisticated because that would be too cold. But for this site, with the natural beauty we have to work with, I think it's the perfect mix of modern and comfortable."

Above: Everything has a place in the kitchen—pepper, utensils, even electricity. Two outlets hide beneath panels on the island.
Right: A delicate paper chandelier offers a stunning contrast against the kitchen's sturdy island, which thoughtfully orients the cook toward stunning landscape views.

A smart,
streamlined
layout
makes this
kitchen cook,
yet there's
still room
for artful
displays.

Pretty &
Purposeful

Cabinets and open shelving are blended for decorative value and ease of use. Dual islands offer ample work space while facilitating traffic flow.

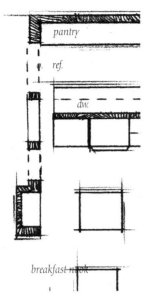

pantry

ref.

dw.

breakfast nook

Right: Display cubbies accessed by a rolling ladder frame the breakfast nook, which strikes a casual note with a built-in bench and vintage chairs covered in floral fabric.
Opposite: A stainless-steel shelf above the cooktop keeps oils and seasonings handy, while open drawers below provide easy access to beautiful cookware.

Seen in the proper perspective, everyday objects can be works of art. That was the thinking behind this Cannon Falls, Minnesota, kitchen that makes beautiful focal points of collectibles ranging from colorful ceramics to lacy linens. Mixing prominent display space with basic paneled cabinets, the deceptively simple architecture allows the collections to shine. Yet, as the displays catch the eye, this design focuses squarely on function.

Architect Todd Hansen envisioned the space for a pair of consummate hosts. The couple wanted a room to hold intimate, casual meals and formal dinner parties for 20 with equal ease. Hansen offered them versatility and efficiency with an open floor plan and elements that hark back to early 20th-century homes. "I've always loved the working areas of older homes—the scullery, laundry rooms, working kitchens, and serving quarters," he says. "Their pure utility has a spareness that, today, seems modern."

Hansen drew on older styles executed "in a modern way," he says. Inspired by traditional raised-panel cabinetry, for example, he used broader proportions and sleek stainless-steel handles to modernize the look. Large-format subway tile also updates the appearance.

An off-white hue on upper cabinets, paired with a French gray below, serves as an ideal backdrop for the colorful bowls on display. "We knew there would be an open storage component to the kitchen, so we kept the color palette fairly neutral," Hansen says. "One of the goals was to have decoration come from the objects themselves."

In Detail

This kitchen's many custom-designed spaces turn basic storage needs into opportunities for adding unique decorative flourishes.

Opposite: A sliding door reveals the contrast between the soft-hue kitchen and the bold-color pantry and closes to hide dirty dishes from guests.

Clockwise, from top left: A swinging door opens to the bold graphic of wine cubbies tucked into a passageway just off the kitchen, outside the main work area but within easy reach. • A glass-front cabinet in the hallway between the kitchen and pantry showcases antique table linens, each neatly hung on dowels and tagged with its size. • An open shelf in one island displays colorful bowls on a vintage bench.

Left: A refrigerator and cabinets, all with stainless-steel doors, are grouped with the wall ovens for impact. Shelves on the same wall, also in stainless steel, display collectibles in hues that match the pantry behind the pass-through with pocket door. Opposite: Stainless steel brings industrial utility to the cleanup zone's countertops and updates a farmhouse sink.

Hansen divided floor-to-ceiling cabinets into task-specific zones. He sheathed a cleanup area in stainless steel, added a lower island topped with maple butcher block to serve as a prep area near the refrigerator and ovens, and designated a large island near the cooktop for gathering and serving.

Open shelves for display dot each zone, from the bottom tier of the marble-topped island to cubbies over the portal framing a breakfast nook. The cubbies are accessed via an old-fashioned library ladder for extra vintage charm.

Additional storage and work zones support the kitchen's primary cooking and gathering space. Each is executed, of course, with a flair for display. Table linens on dowel rods in a glass-front cabinet bring interest to a short hall connecting the kitchen and pantry. And a sliding door built into the

backsplash near the refrigerator offers a glimpse into the boldly painted pantry beyond. A point of visual interest, the sliding door is also useful when entertaining. "The home-owners wanted a way for dishes to disappear after dinner without guests volunteering to help," Hansen says.

The pantry offers beautiful storage and service with an extra sink and dishwasher. The homeowners use this area for staging and cleanup while entertaining in the main kitchen. Bold color in the pantry—including apple-green paint on the cabinets and robin's-egg blue on walls—adds a sense of playfulness, proving that utility can be beautiful.

"Our goal is the integration of function and style," says Hansen, who chose each detail, from varying countertop surfaces to the placement of display niches, to enhance livability and delight the eye. "We saw every need of this kitchen as a design opportunity." 🄱🄺

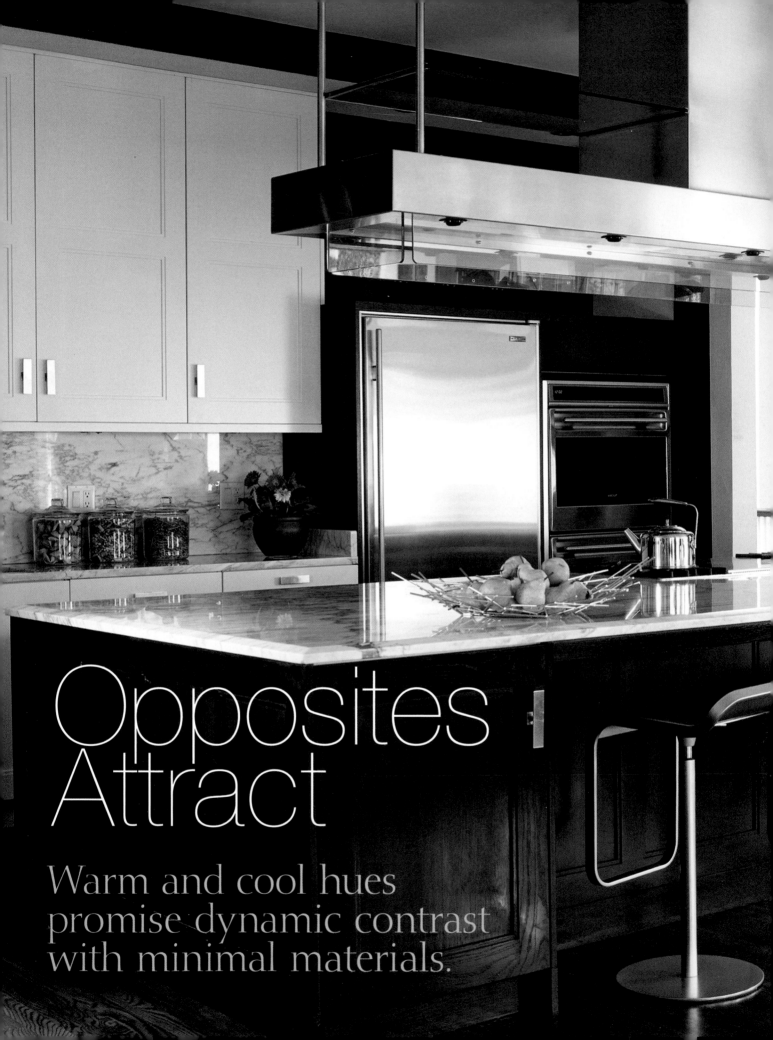

Opposites Attract

Warm and cool hues promise dynamic contrast with minimal materials.

A custom island hood echoes the geometry of this kitchen. Dark wood plays warm counterpoint to cool stainless steel, white painted cabinets, and gleaming carrara marble.

WHY LIMIT YOUR PALETTE?

Kitchens with limited color can achieve these architectural goals, says designer Debra Toney.

UNITY: Repeating the same three materials helped Debra ease transitions from work spaces to dining areas and beyond (the pantry and mudroom). The expanse of adjacent spaces now reads as one.

FOCUS: By limiting color, Debra shifted focus to details, such as shape and texture—for example, marble's polish, steel's cool reflections, or the custom range hood's striking geometry.

DRAMA: It's as simple as black and white. A room with two contrasting hues builds eye-catching drama.

A rainbow of colors held no appeal for residential designer Debra Toney and architect Mark Adcock, who insisted on only classic white, rich browns, and stainless steel in their Denver kitchen. Within that limited palette, the couple found ample opportunity for drama. The key, they say, lay in the proportions and placement of each material. Contrasting light and dark cabinets, and pairing traditional marble with sleek metal accents, the couple created a rhythmic play of hues and styles. The first impression is one of simplicity, while details reveal the sophistication of a custom design.

Opening to an adjoining family room, the 26x14-foot cooking area is part of an extensive addition that adds a refreshingly modern vibe to the home's traditional 1940s architecture. The ample space allows for several hands in meal preparation. "Our family can work and gather together within the same space, which was our big goal," Debra says.

An oversize island (13 feet long and almost 6 feet wide) serves as the kitchen's primary prep and cooking area, providing an ample expanse of countertop space as well as a host of convenient storage features. At the island's center is a powerful cooktop with a French burner. Generous aisles—almost 5 feet wide—ensure that Debra, Mark, and company can move easily around each other and around the island, Mark says. And grouping the sink and

Opposite: The cooktop boasts traditional gas burners and a French burner, which can heat to different temperatures on one surface. The pantry door's frosted-glass panels reflect light but obscure contents.
Above: Stainless steel contemporizes an apron-front sink and continues onto the countertops and backsplash for hardworking elegance. The pro-style faucet adds sculptural interest.

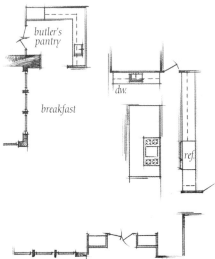

Left: The butler's pantry is open to the kitchen, just steps away from dining. The room is beautifully equipped for coffee or cocktails thanks to an espresso machine, a wine cooler, bar sink, open shelves for glassware, and two refrigerator drawers.
Opposite: Built-in bookshelves run the length of a kitchen wall, framing the doorway to a potting room. Furnished with books and accessories, the shelves bring the kitchen the well-furnished look of a living space.

dishwashers on a separate wall creates a distinct cleanup zone that allows several people to work alongside those at the island.

Though the kitchen was built to be a hub of activity, its aesthetic aims for relaxed elegance through a careful mix of materials. Espresso-stained cabinetry features clean-lined doors that set a rich, contemporary tone, Debra says. Sleek stainless-steel appliances and a stainless countertop and backsplash enhance the sleek, modern feel while adding everyday functionality. Against this dramatic backdrop of dark wood and steel, Debra strategically placed classic materials—white painted cabinetry and carrara marble—that soften the space and inject a sense of familiarity.

The result is a room filled with layers of contrast, which has a surprisingly cohesive feel. "Rhythm is my focus," Debra says. "In my work, I like to limit the number of materials and colors used and concentrate instead on how their placement can build visual rhythm and a sense of continuity within the space" (see sidebar, page 99).

Knowing she wanted to work with contrasting cabinetry colors, for example, she limited her countertop materials to two, with matching backsplashes, for a seamless blend of counter and wall.

The cabinetry and marble carry into the butler's pantry to unify the two rooms. Located where the original kitchen once stood, the pantry connects the kitchen's casual eating area with the formal dining room and serves as a handy beverage center. "It's a nice transition between the new house and the old," Mark says. Plus, it frees family to enjoy a cup of coffee or a glass of wine without intruding on the kitchen's main work area.

With a wall of books for living room ease and a round table between the cooking zone and pantry, the kitchen now easily accommodates everything from quiet meals to impressive catered events. The ability to live informally inside an elegant, contemporary design is at the heart of Debra and Mark's satisfaction with the room's feel and function. "It's absolutely perfect for our family," Mark says. 🕮

Pale yellow color and lustrous surfaces reflect the sunny disposition of an upper-level kitchen using windows as a backsplash.

A Place in the Sun

A soft yellow kitchen makes light of its deft, linear design.

Knowing how much time she planned to spend in the kitchen of her new house, San Diego homeowner and avid cook Linda Sakane had a special request. "I wanted the kitchen to have the best views," she says.

Collaborating with architect John Nalevanko, she opted to build all living spaces, including the kitchen, on the upper level to take in the site's spectacular vistas. Cabinetry still lines every wall, but thanks to windows used in lieu of a back-splash, the cook works amid a 180-degree panorama spanning downtown San Diego, the Pacific Ocean, northern Mexico, and even the Coronado Bridge on a clear day.

Sunny yellow lacquered contemporary cabinetry, stainless-steel accents, and skylights above amplify light in the new kitchen aerie. Says Nalevanko, "The higher elevation allowed us to bring in additional light. Now the room looks sunny even on a day that's gray with a coastal marine layer."

Factoring in the effects of shifting sunlight, Nalevanko gave considerable thought to refinements in hue and tone. Pale yellow cabinets in a flat, almost glasslike finish exude a sun-drenched warmth subtler than bright, glossy options. Flecks of gold seen on the white oak flooring and granite countertops also soften the design's hard lines. The result, Nalevanko says,

Opposite: Cushion-shape sinks bring a few soft lines to a rectilinear design that features a stainless-steel display shelf artfully sited amid cabinets.
Below: The glass-door wine cabinet breaks up a field of stainless steel to display a cache of bottles.

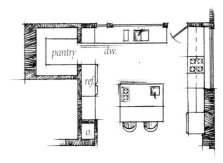

The above-counter window features a deep sill to hold additional countertop items and a mitered glass corner for a wraparound vista.

In Detail

This kitchen uses only four materials—steel, glass, granite, and lacquer—in a variety of rhythmic combinations to maximize perceptions of space and light.

Clockwise from opposite, upper left: A polished finish complements the slick, minimalist faucet design. • Puck lights, installed on the underside of cabinets, illuminate a hammered sterling silver pitcher and glassware chosen with the kitchen's glowing color scheme in mind. • Tucked in gray flannel to thwart tarnish, fine silver rests in one of 15 drawers designed for holding utensils, plastic wrap, and odds and ends. • Lustrous industrial elements, including this dish rack, add to the aesthetic as much as coordinating tablewares. • Resting on a slab of granite, the appliance garage closes with stainless-steel slide-in doors to guarantee a clean look, and no bumped elbows, even when in use. • Textured glass fronts on select cabinets diffuse light in contrast to their highly reflective stainless-steel frames. • The same simple stainless-steel hardware carries over to both cabinet types to unite the two-tone scheme.

"is soothing and gives the kitchen a timeless quality even though it is undeniably contemporary. Linda and her husband, Akira, will be able to live with it for a long time."

Linda and Nalevanko asked kitchen designer Mia Fortescue to plan the cabinetry design and bring their material choices into a workable scheme. She designed the lacquer surfaces to wrap around corners, creating a seamless effect. Specialized storage units abound, all of them opening flush with cabinets. She even accommodated Linda's favorite passion, cooking the labor-intensive meals her Japanese-born husband enjoyed as a youth, with custom cubbies. These include an easily accessible drawer for sushi knives as well as two burners on the island where Linda can cook with a wok while friends and family gather round. And because the home's upside-down plan presents a longer walk from the car, Fortescue added a dumbwaiter to bring up groceries from the garage.

Lastly, windows behind the sink overlook a Zen-style garden. Says Linda, "I learned that I don't live 'in' a home, but rather 'with' it. Nature underscores the ultramodern design of the house, with the kitchen at its center." ✦

Opposite: Wrapping walls and corners in yellow lacquer yields a crisp, clean look that smooth surfaces amplify.
Below: The walk-in pantry is strategically sited just steps away from the prep counter and refrigerator and can be closed off with a space-saving pocket door.

Global

Influence

*J*ust look beyond borders to instill a kitchen with worldly character. Rough-hewn limestone floors and skim-troweled walls that suggest plaster can evoke European panache. Or employ clean, minimalist detailing to conjure Asian tranquillity. These kitchens show that global-inspired design is an exciting adventure that can transport you virtually anywhere.

French Finesse

Discriminating detail
captures the timeless
allure of Provence.

Abundant, free-flowing space allows friends and family to gather frequently in the kitchen, invited by fireside cooking and a strong connection to the outdoors.

Right: Double ovens are set at counter height into a pantry-type arrangement of shelves. The new cabinets have lean lines to update the paneled style of salvaged doors from France, now hinged to fold open and reveal a pass-through to the dining room.

Below: Details ranging from window latch mechanisms to gracefully arched faucets with separate cold and hot water handles channel vintage European style.

Opposite: The marble-top table is a popular meeting place, and an ideal surface for the homeowner to exercise her skill as a pastry chef.

*T*rue collectors have a discerning eye for authenticity. This kitchen, built for a connoisseur of all things French, offers a clean slate for displaying French antiques while also capturing the essence of its inspiration. Under a facade of salvaged boiserie and various other collections, the room is basic and hardworking, with plain white cabinetry and simple hardware—a design so fundamental it could fit into almost any time, any place. What transforms the French-inspired space are layers of carefully chosen fittings and artfully arranged objects. The room takes on a personality that mirrors the homeowner's frequent travels to Provence and her almost native understanding of the *je ne sais quoi* that sets French provincial decor apart.

"The homeowner has an incredible eye for the smallest, most telling detail," says Rob Philabaum, the general contractor with builders G.M. Hunt, Inc., who executed this vision of southern France in suburban Phoenix. "She knew precisely what she wanted." The limestone floor is the most obvious evocation of a French *manoir*. The rough-hewn 17th-century stone from Burgundy lends its age and sense of permanence to the home's new construction.

Tall, double French doors and broad casement windows flood the kitchen and adjacent sunroom with natural light. The latching mechanisms are like those used in old French houses to secure doors and shutters: Handles turn the metal rods that run from top to bottom of each panel frame.

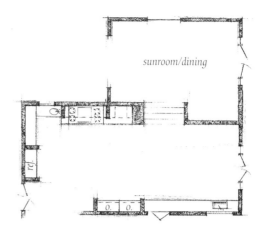

sunroom/dining

Left: A sunroom for casual dining is open to the kitchen and furnished with a similar emphasis on cool whites and naturally worn finishes.
Below: Like many European kitchens, this one has few wall-mount cabinets, leaving space for decoration.
Opposite: A simple strip of molding creates the suggestion of a mantel over the cooking niche, where a modern cooktop joins an open wood-burning oven.

No granite-topped island would suit such a precisely accented space, where even basic work surfaces aim for a distinct Euro spin. A pair of open-sided, ironwork post office tables from France serve as islands instead, their almost industrial look posing a novel contrast to the room's emphasis on art and objects. Stainless-steel surfaces surrounding the pro-style range strike another industrial note. By contrast, the butler's sink next to the steel-topped work area is an antique marble basin decorated with delicately carved arabesques.

The homeowner's dedication to collecting is evident on every surface, from the neatly folded vintage table linens to antique copper cookware nestled among Chinese export porcelain, French faience, ironstone crockery, and antique apothecary jars. White dinner plates, serving bowls, and teacups stacked against etched glassware also jostle for display space. A luminous mirror, with a frame made from architectural salvage, hangs at one end of the kitchen, where the designer eschewed upper cabinets. Such details are applied as though generations of a family passed through the home, each adding its signature.

Most dining happens in the small sunroom that opens off the kitchen. Its architectural details, including an arched window and terra-cotta floor slabs set in a herringbone pattern, are typical of a room dedicated to raising plants. The open metalwork chairs convey an indoor-outdoor setting, but the heavy pine table says "country kitchen."

"The place is full of warmth and character," Philabaum says. "It feels like it's been here for decades. It's unique." 🔳

Right: Contemporary cabinets and Asian elements, including open basket storage and the island's dark, blocky stools, share an emphasis on simplicity.

Asian art collectors find serenity in the sleek detailing of this exquisite kitchen.

Culinary Haiku

Kitchen designer Mick De Giulio has been in the business long enough to take praise in stride. Industry insiders and clients agree the Chicago designer's kitchens are aesthetically pristine and flawlessly engineered. And they handle like a dream. But can they rival art? The streamlined contemporary kitchen he designed for a newly blended Chicago family of art collectors put his talents to the task.

"They just wanted a lot of elbow room so everyone could hang out together," De Giulio says. "The kitchen was large to begin with, but we were able to build out an additional 5 feet into the yard overlooking the pool." He

reused the original floor-to-ceiling windows while capturing extra space for a breakfast table that seats eight. Architect Tony Grunsfeld, known for his minimalist style, oversaw the expansion.

While enlarging the space, De Giulio also redefined its style, taking the homeowners' Asian art collection as inspiration. "We wanted something simple and gallerylike in feeling to pay tribute to their art," he says. On the storage wall, De Giulio retained the original modern windows at the crown of the 10-foot ceiling for a peek at the treetops, then gutted everything below. The new storage is as

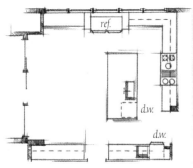

Opposite: The 1930s-style La Cornue range is a "jewel box," designer Mick De Giulio says. A pot filler is part of the kitchen's high-performance function.
Right: The cleanup station includes a sink and a dishwasher discreetly enclosed behind cabinets. Upper cabinets in stainless steel blend well with the stone counters and backsplash. Their frosted-glass doors cloud views for a soft effect.

succinct and serene as haiku. All magnolia-white lacquer sans hardware, it includes a sleek food pantry and cabinets that wrap around two walls. The subtle cabinetry seamlessly segues into the walls and ceiling, which are painted with a custom-color, hand-trawled pearlized linen.

The centerpiece of the storage wall—and the major mood-setter for the kitchen—is the refrigerator, a work of art on the outside with state-of-the-art function inside. "Onto a custom wooden casing, I had an artist emulate the 300-year-old artwork from a red chinoiserie table I have in

my own house," the designer says. Then he commissioned custom hardware for the piece, which features a rich red color that warms and grounds the space. "We were trying to create a kitchen that was sleek with high-gloss lacquer cabinets, but that was toned down by the other elements," De Giulio says.

The breakfast table's impressive craftsmanship rivals that of the refrigerator. Made of cotto pesto—terra-cotta that has been fired and colored—the Italian tabletop's graphics depict a poem about the relationship of the

Opposite: Custom refrigerator drawer and door pulls project the armoire's Asian inspiration.
Above: The stainless-steel island features olive-wood baskets for a warm textural counterpoint.
Right: A bank of clerestory windows catches light while easing the visual flow from the refrigerator to the food pantry on the left and the hanging cabinets on the right. The absence of hardware on all but the fridge ensures the appliance's custom casing as a focal point.

stars and moons. De Giulio purchased the tabletop from an artisan in Bologna, Italy, then commissioned a bronze Parsons-style base. "The Barbara Barry rattan chairs give it an Asian feeling," he says.

A 1930s-style stainless-steel range and island, plus smooth planes of granite on countertops and backsplashes, continue the streamlined look. But even here, textural accents add warmth. "Baskets built into the island are made of olive wood. They, along with bookshelves on the island's other end, take away some of the chill of stainless steel," De Giulio says.

Lighting is minimal and artful, with handblown pendants above the breakfast table and overhead halogen can lights, trim-free and mounted flush with drywall for gallery effect.

It's those tiny warm details that lift the kitchen from a too-cool, adults-only sensibility to a room that's family friendly. But make no mistake: When the entertaining begins, this kitchen wows—and maybe even aspires to art. 🔳

Opposite: The tabletop, made of fired and colored terra-cotta by an Italian artisan, illustrates a poem about celestial music.
Right: A quartet of handblown glass pendants suspended above the custom bronze-base cotto-pesto table is unobtrusive yet inventively modern.

Tuscan Tailored

Old-world charm exudes modern attitude in this artfully designed kitchen.

This photo: Hand-forged iron nails add to the graphic appeal of a coffered refrigerator cabinet.
Opposite: A stunning marble mosaic clads the wall behind the range. The hammered-copper hood is bordered in stainless steel.

Mediterranean architecture has innate grandeur. How, then, can it feel cozy? Or modern? Architectural designer Lynn Sears explored these questions while creating this kitchen within the old-world environment of a Tuscan-style house in Dallas. While honoring the new home's 1920s villa feel, she had to create 21st-century convenience, function, and durability to suit a family of six—including four children who are learning to cook.

"It was a tall order," Sears says. But she met the challenge designing Tuscan charm into a multitasking space. A vast marble-mosaic wall seems almost ancient, while distressed terra-cotta floor tiles resemble old Italian ones. Decorative grillwork graces the hammered-copper range hood, and iron scrollwork dresses up the doorway transoms. The walls are coated with faux Venetian plaster. Graceful arches appear in windows, doorways, and niches. Perhaps most striking, the ceiling undulates with coves in clay-tile veneer crafted to look like old brick, separated by rustic reclaimed beams.

Spare upper cabinetry and a row of three tall arched windows keep the room feeling light, despite its wealth of earthy materials. A large, wide island stores what might have been kept up high. "Having the storage lower just makes sense," Sears says. "It offers easy access to pots and pans."

Appliances cleverly concealed in the cabinetry support the family's frequent culinary endeavors. These include two dishwashers, a pro-grade refrigerator, a snack refrigerator, an icemaker, and a microwave. A six-burner cooktop with grill, three ovens, and a warming drawer are, by contrast, exposed in stainless steel.

The design and its amenities are meant to impress, but not overly so. Sears wanted the room to be elegant but not intimidating—"grand without being grandiose," she says. 🄱🄺

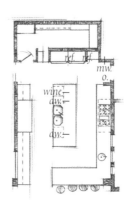

Left: Rustic materials are put to elegant use in this Mediterranean-style kitchen, where activities revolve around a 12×4-foot island full of storage and appliances. A long peninsula separates cooking and prep spaces from the breakfast area.

In Detail

Materials traditional to Mediterranean architecture—mosaic tile, coarse woods, brass, wrought iron, and terra-cotta—are used with distinction.

Opposite: The marble wall mosaic continues around triple arched windows. Yellow painted trim emphasizes each elegant arch and has the refreshing effect of bouncing sunlight into a room filled with earthy hues.

Clockwise, from top: The wall mosaic pattern is centered above the range, where a playful trompe l'oeil of three urns includes large, solid pieces of rare colored marble. • New terra-cotta floor tiles feature an aged, honed surface and interlocking decorative edges. • Reclaimed beams and a veneer of clay tiles form a graceful coved ceiling.

A row of arches distinguishes the kitchen within the great-room. Walls are extra-thick and skim-troweled to suggest solid plaster.

With Spanish Eyes

Rich, subdued color; honed surfaces; and a collected look echo the earthy elegance of Spanish Colonial design.

Getaway trips to a Santa Barbara resort filled kitchen designer Kevin Spearman with a taste for the mystique of Spanish Colonial interiors. Thick, battlement-style walls; candle-flame, iron chandeliers; and marble slabs with veins as red as a Seville orange were some of the historical details lingering in mind when he returned to his drawing board as principal of Bellacasa Design Associates in Houston. But while Santa Barbara's 1920s-era revival of Spanish Colonial architecture often added layers of romance to its inspiration, Spearman saw the potential for an application of the style's simpler tendencies in the kitchen of Alan and Jamie Carnrite.

"We did a lot of research," Spearman says. "We knew the look of this kitchen would be very different from the Italian Mediterranean style that you see throughout suburban Houston. This is more understated, with cool undertones. It's subtle and purposefully rustic. The modern luxuries had to be hidden, but they are still there. The kitchen needed to be able to work for a modern family."

Indeed, the Carnrites and their three teenage boys take full advantage of the kitchen's spacious layout (about 400 square feet) and broad work spaces. "The boys use all the counter space for making panini, malts, and pizzas," Jamie says. "It's very functional."

The floor plan is based on Santa Barbara's vintage Spanish Revival kitchens, which sited several workstations for servants. Spearman therefore emphasized basic and utilitarian elements in keeping with a room whose function came first. The range, for instance, is on its own wall without surrounding cabinets or a mantel top.

"We wanted it to feel kind of raw, even crude," Spearman says. "When you're dealing with a big kitchen space, the temptation is to fill it up with luxury options, but in this case we let the design be the hero."

Right: Cool blue paint on an oversize island draws eyes to the center of Alan and Jamie Carnrite's Spanish-inspired kitchen. Designer Kevin Spearman eschewed the usual configuration of upper and lower cabinets for furniture-style fittings in a range of forms and finishes.

Handmade Mexican tile tops the broad island with a golden hue also found in the distressed finish of the glass-enclosed cupboards. The farmhouse-style porcelain sink sits under a grouping of small, deeply recessed windows Spearman designed for historical accuracy.

Cabinets built on-site hide appliances that include a refrigerator inside a bonnet-topped armoire and two dishwashers integrated into cabinetry on either side of the sink. Materials are meant to suggest vintage construction–from honed red travertine countertops and saltillo flooring to the walnut side paneling and handmade Mexican tiles dressing the center island.

To give the impression of authentic, thick-plaster walls, Spearman had the builder frame them with space in the middle. An ordinary taped-drywall covering then was skim-troweled to suggest plaster. Yawning, arched doorways–a hallmark of Santa Barbara architecture–lead to a loggia on one end of the kitchen and to an open great-room on the other. Recessed lights illuminate the underside of each arch for drama. Above, rustic cedar beams and antique corbels further the room's airs of authenticity.

Though vintage in feel, the kitchen manages contemporary appeal through proportionality and clean lines, Spearman says. Too often, kitchen floor space and ceiling heights can be out of scale, he says, resulting in a series of architectural tricks. "We didn't use any clipped corners or set things on angles," he says. "The room is almost square, the island is almost square, and materials speak for themselves. This had to be about simple elegance."

Perhaps the kitchen's most distinguishing feature, however, is its break from the typical configuration of upper and lower cabinets. "We talked a lot about the room's volume and how to use cabinets to break up the space," Spearman says. He studied classic furniture styles and worked with the firm's cabinet crew to create individual pieces with antiqued finishes.

"Can you imagine if this kitchen were all brown wood?" he says. "I knew we had to make it as authentic and real as possible–inset panel doors, chunky turned legs on the island, and a cool palette of indigo blue, cream, and terra-cotta instead of the usual Mediterranean reds and oranges."

Jamie says what people notice most about the kitchen is that the cabinets don't match. "And that's what I like best about the design," she says. "It all looks collected, like it's been here forever, not like it is brand-new." ⓑ

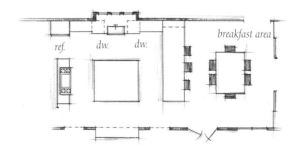

Arched doors leading to a loggia bring drama to the dining area. The chairs and chandelier show the Moorish influence on Spanish Colonial design.

A Perfect Pear
FROM NAPA VALLEY
PEAR BALSAMIC
VINEGAR
NET 16.9 FL. OZ. (500ML)

COLD

*K*itchens may have evolved into comfy, inviting hubs of the home, but peel back the layers and functionality is still at the core. Of course, the 21st-century version of functionality welcomes gourmand indulgences (think pot-filler faucets, pizza ovens, and grand wine refrigerators). These kitchens raise the bar on gracefully melding service with style.

Built on Experience

An expert cabinetmaker with a gourmet streak fashions his dream kitchen.

Opposite: A brick, wood-fired pizza oven sits in the backsplash above the kitchen range. Homeowner Mike Yedowitz assembled the oven core from a kit, then fashioned its brickwork surround. **This photo:** The kitchen features elegant white-painted millwork, much of it custom-made by Mike.

Mike Yedowitz was beginning to feel like the cobbler whose children had no shoes. A building contractor and experienced cabinetmaker, Mike designed and built dream kitchens for clients while he and his wife, Lisa, lived with the spacious but outmoded kitchen of their 1970s ranch house. The 18×23-foot room appeared drab and dark with heavy oak cabinets and a dense overgrowth of trees that crowded right up to its small windows.

The couple gleaned ideas for years until Mike was ready to create something highly personal and unique—but this time for his own family. The result is a hardworking space with a well-conceived plan executed in a style bordering on theatrical.

As an avid cook, Mike knew the importance of lighting. His first order of business was to raise the ceiling height from 8 feet to 13 feet, making way for elegant south-facing transom windows. Outside, trees were removed or heavily pruned. And to amplify the kitchen's newfound pools of natural light, Mike opted for the glow of an all-in-one copper sink and countertop sited beneath the kitchen's ample windows.

Raising the roof high also enabled Mike to create the room's most elaborately crafted element: a double-coffer

Right: Wood countertop surfaces of different heights distribute the mass of the oversize island well, allocating distinct space for gathering at one end and chopping at the other. Cabinets are fitted under the prep side only, while legs support the dining end.

ceiling with decorative beam moldings. Deciding against pendants above the island, Mike hung handcrafted metal chandeliers from the ceiling's lower beams. The uplight reveals the gently sculpted profile of the ceiling coffers.

Once the ceiling and transom windows were completed, Mike focused on the kitchen's layout. He wanted the space to fit the way the couple lives and entertains. During the workweek it's a family haven for Mike, Lisa, and their three sons, ages 10, 8, and 5. On the weekend it's a welcoming space designed for the enjoyment of good food, fine wine, and friendship.

Mike and Lisa share a passion for cooking and entertaining, with the central island as their stage. The area features a bias-cut maple butcher block prep station at one end and countertop dining at the other end. This configuration invites free-flowing conversation between hosts and guests.

Enhancing the room's lived-in feel are cabinets designed to resemble pieces of furniture. An antique-style cherry wardrobe conceals the commercial-grade refrigerator, as well as slide-out spice racks on either side. Niches with arched recesses flanking the working fireplace provide display space for fresh flower arrangements.

Six months after the cabinetry was completed, however, the backsplash behind the range remained unfinished. "The kitchen was so unique that an

Top: Sunlight from windows bounces off copper countertops, enhancing the material's warm glow and richly varied patina.
Right: The custom chopping block's extra thickness distinguishes the island's prep function from its dining/serving zone.
Opposite: Tall transom windows reach the ceiling's new height and flood the kitchen with natural light.

ordinary tile treatment would have been cliché," Mike says. "We needed something special." They found the answer while taking a cooking course near Lucca, in Tuscany. "We cooked dishes in a 250-year-old brick oven—I took one look and knew that a brick surround was the perfect solution," Mike says.

Mike intended to build a genuine brick oven, but his research showed the process would be complicated, even for an experienced contractor. Further online investigation brought Mike to a company that stocks prefabricated units. Available in several sizes and with all component parts provided, the units take some of the risk out of building an oven from scratch. Nevertheless, Mike discovered the project was no small job. "And I'm in the business," he says.

But being in the business is what gave the Yedowitzes the foresight to wait. After all, besides the right contractor, a truly ideal kitchen, Mike says, takes a bit of effort and a well of patience. **BK**

Top: Handsome cherrywood coffered panels conceal the refrigerator with the style of an antique armoire.
Right: Panels also conceal a pair of pullout spice racks flanking the refrigerator.
Opposite: Arched niches, in built-ins designed by Mike, showcase fresh flowers that are a regular part of the kitchen's decor.

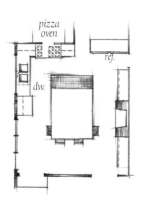

This photo: Every detail on the range and hood is customized, from the color and oven size to the burner layout and brushed-brass trim and pot rail. **Opposite:** A refrigerator cabinet is styled to look freestanding, much like the range, which is sited between a baker's table and a butcher-block table with knife slots.

Period details are spotlighted and modern amenities cleverly tucked away in this 1926 kitchen.

Heritage on Display

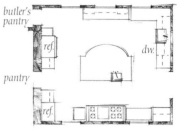

Left: The butler's pantry boasts refurbished cabinets and original elements including a chestnut countertop, silver-alloy sink, and reconditioned latches and pulls.
Opposite: Creamy-hue lower cabinets and the smooth black granite of the sink, countertop, and camelback backsplash offer sharp contrast to the new plate rack, which has dark stain, beefy molding, and Victorian-style dowels that pose as antique.

History imbued this kitchen with warmth. Fir flooring and plaster walls spoke to its pedigree as part of a country estate near Red Bank, New Jersey. Terra-cotta tiles were crackled with age, and the slate hearth in the kitchen and silver-alloy sink in the butler's pantry were original to the 1926 home.

Heritage? The kitchen had plenty of it. But modern conveniences were in short supply. With preservation in mind, the homeowners hired David Chiarella, a certified kitchen designer (CKD) and member of the National Kitchen & Bath Association (NKBA).

Chiarella's mission was to outfit the kitchen for contemporary living while staying true to its stately past. "Back then, these rooms had worktables, a sink station, and a freestanding range," he says. "Kitchens were somewhat unfitted—not the built-in look common today."

Using fine finishes and beautiful crafting, Chiarella obscured the line between old and new. The china hutch, for instance, was built around an existing window. "We wanted it to look like it was always there," he explains.

In lieu of counters, a freestanding baker's table and a butcher-block table flank the range. Both sit lower than counter height to accommodate original windows. A fetching wall-mount plate rack in richly stained walnut above the sink and banks of glass-front china storage designed to resemble breakfronts also contribute to a historic, unfitted look.

Perimeter cabinets change in depth and character for the historical feel of a vintage unfitted kitchen, and for clear distinctions among cooking, prep, cleanup, and dining zones.

The range, a French model in pistachio green, is a showstopper with a customized layout of griddle, grill, and both gas and electric burners. Considering the home's history, Chiarella knew just where to site it. "Homes of this period put those big old ranges on a flush slab of slate to catch sparks," he says. "That told me exactly where this range should go—with the home's original white glazed terra-cotta tiles for a backdrop."

A thick slab of honed limestone tops the expansive island that gives the kitchen an eat-in advantage. "I thought rounding it would make it more conducive to conversation, and it helps the traffic flow because the sink is on one side of the kitchen and the refrigerators are on the other," Chiarella says.

The island's design, with a post at each corner, was inspired by the table that probably sat in the kitchen in its early days. "This is supposed to look like a worktable yet accommodate what we need today," Chiarella says.

Keeping the vintage feel of the space sent some appliances undercover, with the dishwasher paneled and the microwave below deck on the island. "Today, typically, people want to panel their refrigerators and make them look like furniture, but I went against that thinking," Chiarella says. "In an old kitchen you would definitely see the refrigerator in all its glory, so why not play up the refrigerators?"

Flanking the entry to the walk-in pantry, the two refrigerator/freezers have a carbon stainless-steel finish. The larger one cools drinks and snacks, while the smaller one—situated closer to the range—handles food storage.

In addition to the walk-in pantry, the kitchen includes a sunny butler's pantry with original glass, hardware, and Art Deco cabinetry. New lattice doors dress up an old but operable plate warmer.

The restoration also preserved a pass-through with a sliding door. "It allowed the servants to pass food and drink to the dining room side," Chiarella says. Like the rest of the kitchen, it's just as functional today as it was close to a century ago, thanks to a penchant for preservation. 🕮

In Detail

The same furniture details that make cabinets ring true to this kitchen's 1920 roots also finely tune pieces to meet contemporary storage needs.

Opposite: Glass-front cabinets displaying tablewares flank an original window to dress this built-in unit as a china breakfront. The unit's handsome walnut counter—at a lower height than nearby granite counters—also furthers the illusion of freestanding furniture.

Clockwise, from top left: Open pullout shelves fitted with willow baskets add old-fashioned style and practical shaded storage for vegetables. • Drawers resembling vintage desk drawers are used to store tea and recipe cards and to underline the original windows. • The old-fashioned worktable emerges in a new form in the massive island. Table legs support the extended countertop for dining, while the island's end drawers hold knives and kitchen tools at the top, place mats in the middle, and lid organizers at the bottom.

An Upper East Side kitchen mixes tradition and pro-style with a sense of family fun.

Metropolitan Medley

This photo: Reminiscent of a retro diner, the texture of a quilted stainless-steel backsplash visually connects the range and exhaust hood. **Opposite:** Calcutta marble is cut 2 inches thick to top the island and work spaces. "Thick countertops are such a statement," homeowner Lois Robbins-Zaro says.

Early memories of baking lessons with her mother or recent praise for keeping the best-stocked pantry on the block—Lois Robbins-Zaro relishes all the comforts of a great family kitchen. "Many of my fondest memories are based in the kitchen," she says. "And so I wanted our own kitchen to be a place where my children and their friends would want to gather."

But as Lois and her husband soon learned, it would be a challenge to transform their apartment's cramped galley into a stylish and hardworking kitchen worthy of their Upper East Side location and that could accommodate the traffic of three kids and three dogs. The couple knocked down walls, subsuming two closet-size spaces. The resulting 24×30-foot kitchen is ample, yet modest considering its many functions.

As Lois bounced around ideas for appliances, materials, and details with interior designer Robert Simon, kitchen designer Linda Dimitriou focused the potentially vast space into a series of zones. Each zone is designed to make the cook feel competent, empowered, and efficient. "Everything has a place," Dimitriou says, "and that makes this kitchen a fun place to work."

A 12-foot-long dark walnut island is the centerpiece. Dimitriou made the most of the island's generous size, finding room for glass-front dry-goods bins, produce baskets, a preparation sink, and generous knee space for barstools.

Right: Traditionally styled cabinets, sumptuous marble and stone, and strategically placed industrial-chic elements blend well inside this free-flowing multizone family kitchen.

Top: A lean column of open cubbies organizes baking supplies next to the stacked microwave, wall oven, and warming drawer.

Above: A section of walnut-stained cabinets serves as a beverage center complete with a bar sink, a built-in espresso maker, coffee grinders, and a refrigerated drawer for cream and other extras. A chalkboard provides a family message center on the nearby utility closet door.

Above right: Arched doors below the stainless-steel farmhouse sink and glass-front cabinets above distinguish the cleanup zone, also used as a secondary food-prep zone. Shiny nickel bin pulls and latches add a vintage touch.

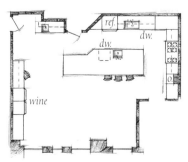

The far corner of the kitchen houses the cooking zone: a six-burner gas range with grill, along with two ovens, a microwave, and a warming drawer. Ample cold storage is sited throughout the space, with the main refrigerator near a glass-front display cabinet, a secondary refrigerator in an adjacent pantry, and a pair of concealed freezer drawers at easy reach in the island (including one dedicated entirely to the family's passion for ice cream). A deluxe coffee-and-dessert station adjacent to the utility door is convenient to diners but isolated from the fray of meal preparation and cleanup.

Industrial-chic touches complement the room's classic maple cabinets and 2-inch-thick Calcutta marble countertops. The most notable is a quilted stainless-steel backsplash like those found behind vintage lunch counters. Reproduction light fixtures over the island and a restaurant-style coiled hand-sprayer add to the room's professional styling.

Furnishings provide the final touch to a kitchen that can handle serious cooking as well as dinner parties. "It's simply a great hangout place," Lois says. "We love this room." ◼

An oversize wine refrigerator and china storage anchor the casual dining area, where rattan furnishings and botanical fabrics introduce soft, nature-inspired texture.

This photo: Each side of the cooking niche houses additional appliances—a microwave and warming drawer at one end and stacked ovens at the other.
Opposite: The custom copper hood and patterned stone backsplash extend across the cooking niche, where pro-grade appliances fit neatly into elegant, furniture-style cabinetry.

Function First

Restaurant efficiency and home-style comforts mix in a kitchen designed for a serious cook.

*T*alent isn't all it takes to cook like a four-star chef. Also required is a kitchen with smooth flow, ample work space, and great function. How that same space can exude all the comforts of home was the question raised by Juli and Keith Jacobs, owners of a Chicago home-building company. The couple wanted the kitchen in their new house to be fit for a pro and brimming with the old-world ambience of their overall home design.

The kitchen had to look a century old yet function for a modern family with young children—and a serious cook. "Cooking is my passion," Juli says. "If I could quit my day job and be a chef, that would be my dream come true."

Working with a generous footprint and a detailed wish list, Juli assembled the best design team she could find to plan the kitchen down to the last cutlery drawer. The team included interior designer Doug Nickless and cabinetry specialist Christine Moritz. "Juli knew she wanted old-world

Above: A sliding door pass-through links the kitchen with a built-in buffet that serves the dining room.
Left: Two islands are equipped for separate tasks. The primary island features a walnut butcher-block top and houses the main sink and dishwasher. Overhead lighting throughout comes from vintage fixtures salvaged from a Chicago school. The stainless-steel door is the entrance to a walk-in cooler holding cases of water and wine, party trays, bulk foods, and flowers.

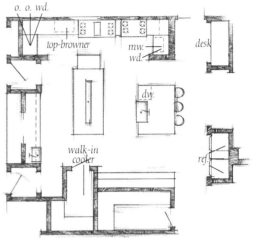

Left: A much-loved 19th-century French butcher block determined the size of the adjacent marble-topped island. "It had to be a showpiece," homeowner Juli Jacobs says.

Opposite: A deep ceramic sink is large enough to wash the indoor barbecue grill. A floor pedal turns on the faucet, and towel bars are strategically placed here and around the kitchen. "I like towels hanging in several places for quick use cleaning and prepping," Juli says.

style and a commercial-quality kitchen," Nickless says. "But our primary goal was to build a multitasking kitchen that could handle traffic." This was accomplished by dividing the space into zones, including a cooking cove, prep zones, and a pass-through service area.

Two islands serve as the heart of the kitchen. The primary island, topped with dark walnut, is designed for dining as well as food preparation. Refrigerator and freezer drawers make it a handy place to fix the children's lunches in the morning. The second island, topped with marble, features a custom nickel sink with a commercial-grade sprayer overhead. Each island's base matches the perimeter cabinetry, which includes one wall of china storage visible through divided-light doors.

Scale builds drama. "All cabinets are stacked to the ceiling," Moritz says, "and the ceilings are 10 feet high." Paneling, wainscoting, crown molding, and vintage-look bin-style pulls and knobs lend cabinetry an established look.

The kitchen's focal point, however, is the cooking cove framed by an arched stone surround. It houses four ovens (two gas and two electric), eight gas burners, an infrared

barbecue grill, a griddle, a top-browner, and an under-counter steamer that Juli uses for everything from crab legs to braised pork. Three 1,500-cfm exhaust fans behind the custom copper hood pull out the heat.

To ensure an efficient arrangement of such diverse cooking appliances, Juli rounded out her team of specialists with professional chef Pete Trusiak. "He helped me find the most logical place for each appliance," Juli says. Trusiak also returned when the kitchen was finished to show the Jacobses and friends how to cook while moving from zone to zone. "My guests were chopping and searing and slicing," Juli says. "We cooked a different course on each appliance."

This kitchen may welcome multiple cooks, but "it's not intimidating for one," Nickless says. Its industrial quality is carefully tempered by such timeless materials as terracotta and marble. "Adding warm materials like nickel and copper offsets the cool stainless steel," Nickless says. "It's industrial, but still old-world."

And that's just how Juli likes it. "As high-tech as it gets, it's still comfortable for making chocolate chip pancakes for the children in the morning," she says. ✦

In Detail

Restaurant-grade amenities are at home in this kitchen thanks to a calibrated mix of industry and comfort. Here are a few of the room's successful blends.

Opposite: Modular refrigeration allows such custom combinations as this fridge, freezer, and storage for cold beverages in between with a decorative glass-front door.
Above: A nickel trough sink takes up little counter space. For parties, the homeowner fills it with ice and bottled beverages. Before guests arrive and after they leave, however, the sink is all about work thanks to an overhead sprayer that discreetly retracts into the ceiling.
Left: Extras in the cooking cove include the French top offering a 22-inch cooking surface on the 60-inch range, a wall-mount browner, and cabinets finished with elegant, furniture-style bracket feet.

All Work & All Play

This kitchen works as hard as a restaurant while serving up a feast for the eyes.

Opposite: A collection of creamware pitchers dresses the table with casual flair.
This photo: The long, rectangular kitchen extends from elegant dining at one end to casual countertop seating at the center and a restaurant-efficient work space at the opposite end.

K itchens with the space and amenities to accommodate professional cooks are often not the coziest of spaces for waking up over morning coffee or snacking over homework. Yet the team at Bellacasa Design Associates in Houston created this showhouse kitchen to be highly efficient and exceptionally inviting for anyone from a busy family to a flurry of caterers.

"We wanted to give this kitchen a very sophisticated and understated appeal, but not in a stark or sterile sense. People want to gather and cook in a livable kitchen, not a characterless laboratory," explains Kevin Spearman, owner of Bellacasa.

To make the workhorse space welcoming, balance was key. "There are equal measures of warm and cool, new and old, high-tech modern and reassuring traditional," Spearman says. Intriguing in combination (and contrast) are the shiny stainless-steel elements (the refrigerator, freezer, and all-in-one sink and counter) and the earthy materials—namely the green slate floor, the ceiling beams reclaimed from an old farmhouse, and the dark walnut-stained wood lower cabinetry.

Recalling many restaurant layouts, the kitchen eschews upper cabinets on either side of the range, refrigerator, and sink area. Open shelves flank the range, adding to the room's

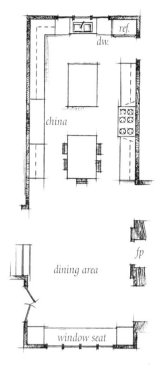

Opposite: With varied heights and depths on the upper cabinetry, built-ins mimic unfitted furniture.
Right: A two-sided fireplace with a hand-carved limestone surround brings warmth and definition to the dining area at one end of the kitchen.

unique aesthetic, and allowing the cook to reach plates swiftly, with one hand. "Open shelves create more of a sophisticated loftlike look," Spearman says.

Whereas the range wall aimed for sleekness, tradition received focal point status on the opposite wall. Here a spacious hutch, featuring a combination of wire grille and glass-pane doors, masquerades as a fine antique.

Two attractive islands also add character while breaking up the long and narrow space. Cabinets underneath make one island utilitarian; space below the other keeps six shapely, upholstered stools out of the way, yet at the ready for guests who like to kibitz with the cook. Both islands are on casters and can be easily moved.

The kitchen's versatility doesn't end with the cooking and prep areas. At the far end of the room, beside a stone fireplace, comfortable upholstered seating pieces and a rustic wood table provide an ideal spot for casual meals. At night, with the chandelier dimmed and the fireplace aglow, the area becomes a cozy enclave, convenient to the kitchen, yes, but also a wonderful world of its own. 🎔

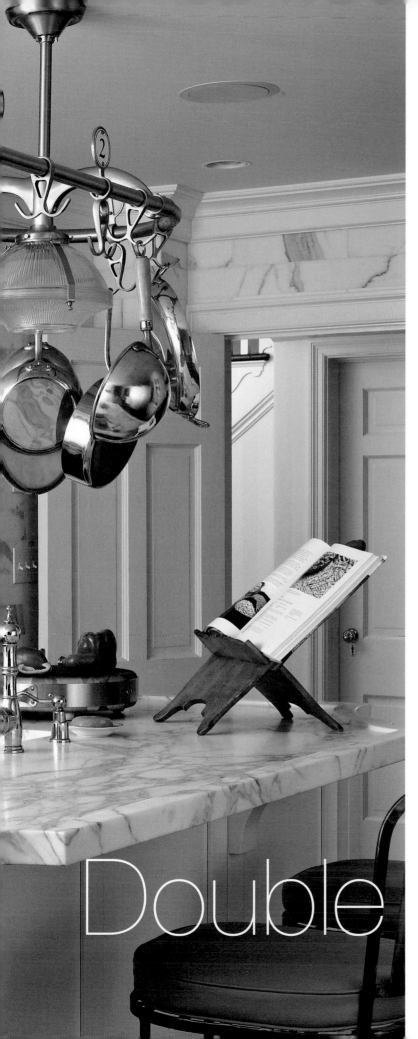

Dual islands give this kitchen distinct cooking and entertaining areas, united by expanses of white marble and steel.

Double Feature

Right: A pilaster next to the brushed and polished stainless-steel range pulls out to reveal handy spice storage.

Opposite: The range area is topped with a striking custom hood that showcases a mix of finishes—stainless steel, and both polished and brushed nickel.

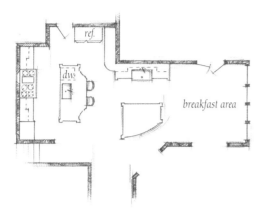

Family and guests love to gather around an island. But in this Scarsdale, New York, kitchen, designer Karen Williams was charged with creating a private cooking space—one where the homeowner could put the finishing touches on dinner without interruption. The challenge, of course, was to meet this desire for cooking in seclusion and still create a welcoming atmosphere for guests.

The answer came in the form of dual islands—one to act as an efficient prep area and the other to serve as a buffet space for casual entertaining. The prep island separates the range and double ovens from the rest of the kitchen and defines the cooking area without cutting it off from the other spaces. The buffet island, meanwhile, elegantly links the cooking area with the breakfast area newly added to the 1930s-era home and doubles as a spot for guests to congregate.

The floor plan successfully achieves all the homeowner's goals, although it came with its own complications. "It was a very difficult space because it was compartmentalized with two separate areas," says Williams, of the firm St. Charles of New York. "To try to make it function as one kitchen was quite challenging."

To unite the two spaces into a cohesive room, she employed a limited palette of materials for cabinetry, countertops, and walls. "We were going for a really clean, crisp look," Williams says, "and the materials are consistent with that." Calcutta marble, with its stunning soft gray veining, for example, brings traditional appeal to both countertops and walls while offering a soft contrast to cabinetry painted a crisp white. Stainless steel and other cool-tone metals complement the marble's grays with a hint of modern style.

This island, one of two in the kitchen, offers a convenient buffet space. The curved side is gracefully echoed in a glass-front cabinet on the opposite wall, which marks the transition from the cooking zone to the cleanup area.

Below: Durable stainless-steel end caps add a modern counterpoint alongside traditional furniture-style feet. Olive knuckle hinges are in keeping with the 1930s home.
Right: The dining addition is dramatically set off by a coffered ceiling and French doors.
Opposite: Marble elevates a traditional apron-front sink in the cleanup area. Its luxurious detailing includes countertops 2 inches thick and a swooping camelback design on the backsplash.

Carefully placed curves attract attention and lead the eye throughout the space. A curved edge on the buffet island gently encourages movement from the kitchen into the adjoining breakfast area, while a curved cabinet near the refrigerator leads eyes around the corner to ease the transition between the cooking area and the cleanup zone. "The beautiful, curved cabinet softens the hard edges and complements the curve on the island," Williams says.

Eye-catching curves also define the sculptural range hood. "I designed it custom in materials that match the kitchen," Williams says. "We needed a strong hood to complement the range." The range combines brushed and stainless steel while the hood seamlessly alternates stainless steel with polished and brushed nickel, echoing the mix of finishes that Williams chose for faucets and cabinet hardware. "If you use the same materials but vary finishes, it creates intriguing texture and dimension," Williams explains.

Small, thoughtful details further enhance the kitchen's charm and function. For hardworking elegance in the cooking zone, Williams installed stainless-steel cabinets on the side of the prep island that faces the range. She continued this detail with stainless-steel caps at the bottom of the cabinetry, a subtle update to the usual pilaster that also eliminates worries of chipping paint. "Aesthetically, it's a very nice detail that's also very functional," Williams says.

She brought new style and practicality to the marble as well. Rather than installing slabs on the walls, Williams cut the marble into thin strips for a look reminiscent of subway tile. On the countertop around the cleanup sink, she created a recessed perimeter to catch splashes. And on the marble backsplash behind, she added a second piece of marble cut into a camelback design. It brings to mind an antique hutch and epitomizes the look of this kitchen: modern approaches to traditional design elements. ◾

In Detail

The same furniture details that make cabinets ring true to this kitchen's 1930s roots also finely tune pieces to meet contemporary storage needs.

Opposite: The range backsplash features marble cut and laid in the style of early 20th-century subway tiles, but with the elegant addition of an arched recessed niche useful for keeping oils and spices in easy reach.
Clockwise, from top left: Marble around the sink is ½ inch lower than the rest of the counter, forming a subtle lip to contain splashes. • A raised edge on the prep island's marble countertop emphasizes its decorative corner treatment, which echoes other curves—including those on the built-in china cabinet behind. • Deep drawers that conform to the curve of the buffet island provide space for entertaining essentials, while an open shelf displays antique platters and blue-and-white china.

resources

Classic Elegance

8-13
Tradition with an Edge

Architect: Ray Murakami, Murakami Design, Inc., Toronto, Ontario; 416/944-9900; *murakamidesign.com*
Builder: Frank Campoli, J.T.F. Homes, Toronto, Ontario; 416/787-1333
Interior designers: Brian Gluckstein and Stephen Wagg, Gluckstein Design Planning, Toronto, Ontario; 416/928-2067

14-19
Lighter, Brighter & Timeless

Residential designer: Robert Dame, Robert Dame Designs, Houston; 713/270-8225
Builder: Tommy Bailey, Tommy Bailey Homes, Inc., The Woodlands, Texas; 281/364-8585
Interior designers: Kelly Welsh and Kevin Spearman, Bellacasa Design Associates, Inc., The Woodlands, Texas; 281/419-5550; *bellacasadesign.com*

20-25
Regal Redux

Architect: Dee Dee Hannah, Dee Dee Taylor Hannah Architect, Inc., Toronto, Ontario; 416/920-7899; *taylorhannaharchitect.com*

26-33
Custom Blend

Residential designer: Robert Dame, Robert Dame Designs; 713/270-8225
Builder: Brian Thompson, Thompson Custom Homes; 832/327-0197; *thompsoncustomhomes.com*
Interior and kitchen designers: Kelly Welsh (interior designer) and Kevin Spearman (kitchen designer), Bellacasa Design Associates Inc.; 281/419-5550; *bellacasadesign.com*

34-39
In Dark & Light

Interior designer: Brian Gluckstein, Gluckstein Design Planning, Toronto, Ontario; 416/928-2067

Relaxed Refinement

42-49
Cottage Sophisticate

Architect: Patrick Ahearn, Ahearn Schopfer Associates, Boston; 617/266-1710; *ahearnschopfer.com*
Builder: Laurence Clancy, West Tisbury, Massachusetts; 508/509-4068
Interior designer: Beverly Ellsley, Beverly Ellsley Design, Westport, Connecticut; 203/454-0503; *beverlyellsley.com*

50-55
Courting Character

Architect: David C. Fowler; *dcfarchitecture.com*
Designer: Laura Walker, Laura Walker Ltd.; *laurawalkerltd.com*

56-61
A Soft Touch

Architect: Stanley McKay & Associates Architects, St. Louis; no further information available

62-69
Natural Embrace
Architect: Lyman Perry, Lyman Perry Architects, Ltd., Berwyn, Pennsylvania; 610/889-9966; *lymanperryarchitects.com*
Interior designer: Jean Courtney Creative Designs, Cambridge, Massachusetts; *jeancourtneycreativedesigns.com*
Contractor: Pete Feldman, Feldman Brothers Construction Co., Chatham, Massachusetts; 508/945-0200
Artist and decorative painter: Eric Karl Andersen, Newburyport, Massachusetts; 617/413-1164

70-77
Pastoral Suite
Kitchen designer: Mick De Giulio, De Giulio Kitchen Design, Inc., Wilmette, Illinois; 847/256-8833; *degiuliokitchens.com*
Interior designer: Mary Ellen Henderson, Henderson Consulting, Inc., Libertyville, Illinois; 847/363-9577

Sleek Sophistication
80-87
Modern Bliss
Architecture firm: Michael Palza (project designer), Hunt Hale Jones; 415/512-1300; *hunthalejones.com*
Designer: Shawn Gillam Associates; 415/456-5010
Contractor: Kerr Construction; 415/662-2188

88-95
Pretty & Purposeful
Architects: Todd Hansen (project architect), Mark Tamborino (project manager), and Christine Albertsson and Sonya Carel (project team members), Albertsson Hansen Architecture, Ltd., Minneapolis; 612/823-0233; *aharchitecture.com*
Builder: Peter McKinnon, River City Builders and Millworks, Inc.; Nerstrand, Minnesota; 507/645-0551; *rcbmi.com*

96-101
Opposites Attract
Architect: Mark Adcock, Debra Toney Residential Design and Development/NAHB, Denver; 303/399 2677; *debratoney.com*
Interior designer: Debra Toney (see above)

102-111
A Place in the Sun
Architect: John Nalevanko, Del Mar, California; 858/481-5638
Cabinet design: Mia Fortescue, Fortescue Design, San Diego
Cabinet installation: Michael Fineman's Kitchen Studio Del Mar, Del Mar, California; 858/350-5995

Global Influence
114-119
French Finesse
Architects: Mark B. Candelaria, Candelaria Design Associates, LLC, Phoenix; *candelariadesign.com*. Oz Architects, Inc., Scottsdale, Arizona; 480/443-4904; *ozarchitects.com*

120-127
Culinary Haiku
Architect: Grunsfeld Shafer Architects, LLC, Evanston, Illinois; 847/424-1800
Kitchen designer: Mick De Giulio, De Giulio Kitchen Design, Inc., Wilmette, Illinois; 847/256-8833; *degiuliokitchens.com*
Interior designer: Suzanne Lovell, Suzanne Lovell, Inc., Chicago; 312/595-1980; *suzannelovellinc.com*

128-133
Tuscan Tailored
Architectural designer: Lynn Sears, Lynn Sears Interiors, Inc.; 214/521-9717; *lynnsearsinteriors.com*
General contractor: Randy Clowdus Construction; 214/366-2233

134-141
With Spanish Eyes
Architectural designer: Robert Dame, Robert Dame Designs, Houston; 713/270-8225
Builder: Robin Rueby, Rueby Custom Homes, Kingwood, Texas; 281/358-7961; *ruebycustomhomes.com*
Interior designer: Kevin Spearman, Bellacasa Design Associates, Inc., The Woodlands, Texas; 281/419-5550; *bellacasadesign.com*

Chef's Specials
144-151
Built on Experience
Designer-builder: Michael Yedowitz, BARC, LLC, Bridgewater, Connecticut; 860/350-0292

152-159
Heritage on Display
Design team: David Chiarella (kitchen designer), Kevin Calver (assistant designer), Peggy Chiarella (assistant designer), Joseph Parisi (kitchen decorator), Kevin Calver Sr. (kitchen installer), and Joe Skelly (kitchen installer), Creative Kitchens, Red Bank, New Jersey; 732/842-2331

160-165
Metropolitan Medley
Kitchen designer: Linda Dimitriou, St. Charles of New York, Inc., New York City; 212/838-2812; *stcharlesofnewyork.com*
Interior designer: Robert Simon, Simon-Van Hoover Associates, New York City; 212/758-0335

166-173
Function First
Interior designer: Doug Nickless, Doug Nickless, Inc., Chicago; 312/755-1855

174-179
All Work & All Play
Architectural designer: Robert Dame, Robert Dame Designs, Houston; 713/270-8225
Builder: Brian Thompson, Thompson Custom Homes, Houston; 713/203-5150
Interior designer: Kevin Spearman, Bellacasa Design Associates, The Woodlands, Texas; 281/419-5550

180-189
Double Feature
Kitchen designer: Karen Williams, St. Charles of New York, Inc., New York City; 212/838-2812; *stcharlesofnewyork.com*

find your style

Decorative paint
Techniques & Ideas

BATH Design Guide

NEW COLOR SCHEMES MADE EASY

POPULAR PALETTES FOR EVERY ROOM

The **elements** of your style can be found in great decorating books from Better Homes and Gardens®